Physical Characteristics of the Black and Tan Coonhound

(from the American Kennel Club breed standard)

Back: The back is level, powerful and strong.

Tail: The tail is strong, with base slightly below level of backline, carried free and when in action at approximately right angle to back.

Hindquarters: Quarters are well boned and muscled. From hip to hock long and sinewy, hock to pad short and strong. Stifles and hocks well bent and not inclining either in or out. When standing on a level surface, the hind feet are set back from under the body and the leg from pad to hock is at right angles to the ground.

Size: Measured at the shoulder—Males 25 to 27 inches; females 23 to 25 inches.

Coat: The coat is short but dense to withstand rough going.

Color: As the name implies, the color is coal black with rich tan markings above eyes, on sides of muzzle, chest, legs and breeching, with black pencil markings on toes.

Black and Tan Coonhound

By Linda Hibbard

Contents

9   **History of the** Black and Tan Coonhound

Although its roots may lie across the Atlantic Ocean, the Black and Tan Coonhound is truly an all-American breed, refined in the United States' southern region. Uncover the breed's ancestors, both foreign and domestic, as well as the breeders who gave rise to this wonderful scenthound. Also discussed are the recognition of the Black and Tan Coonhound by the AKC and UKC and the breed's history in show.

21   **Characteristics of the** Black and Tan Coonhound

From hunting to show competition to companionship, the Black and Tan Coonhound is a multitalented breed that will make an all-purpose canine companion. Discover what makes the Black and Tan the ideal hunting partner as well as what kind of home is best suited for this loyal and loving hound. Also learn about health issues that are pertinent to this breed.

28 **Breed Standard for the** Black and Tan Coonhound

Learn the requirements of a well-bred Black and Tan Coonhound by studying the description of the breed set forth in the American Kennel Club standard. Both show dogs and pets must possess key characteristics as outlined in the breed standard.

36   **Your Puppy** Black and Tan Coonhound

Find out about how to locate a well-bred Black and Tan Coonhound puppy. Discover which questions to ask the breeder and what to expect when visiting the litter. Prepare for your puppy-accessory shopping spree. Also discussed are home safety, the first trip to the vet, socialization and solving basic puppy problems.

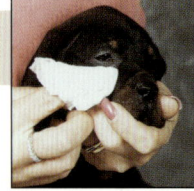

60   **Proper Care of Your** Black and Tan Coonhound

Cover the specifics of taking care of your Black and Tan Coonhound every day: feeding for the puppy, adult and senior dog; grooming, including coat care, ears, eyes, nails and bathing; and exercise needs for your dog. Also discussed are the essentials of dog identification.

Training Your Black and Tan Coonhound   80

Begin with the basics of training the puppy and adult dog. Learn the principles of house-training the Black and Tan Coonhound, including the use of crates and basic scent instincts. Get started by introducing the pup to his collar and leash and progress to the basic commands. Find out about obedience classes and other activities.

Healthcare of Your Black and Tan Coonhound   101

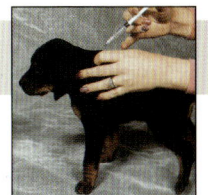

By Lowell Ackerman DVM, DACVD
Become your dog's healthcare advocate and a well-educated canine keeper. Select a skilled and able veterinarian. Discuss pet insurance, vaccinations and infectious diseases, the neuter/spay decision and a sensible, effective plan for parasite control, including fleas, ticks and worms.

Showing Your Black and Tan Coonhound   130

Step into the center ring and find out about the world of showing pure-bred dogs. Here's how to get started in AKC shows, how they are organized and what's required for your dog to become a champion. Take a leap into the realms of obedience trials, agility and hunting tests.

Behavior of Your Black and Tan Coonhound   146

Analyze the canine mind to understand what makes your Black and Tan Coonhound tick. The following potential problems are addressed: aggression (fear-biting, inter-canine and dominant), separation anxiety, digging, barking and food-related problems.

Index 156

KENNEL CLUB BOOKS® BLACK AND TAN COONHOUND
ISBN-13: 978-1-59378-393-8

Copyright © 2009 • Kennel Club Books® • A Division of BowTie, Inc.
40 Broad Street, Freehold, NJ 07728 USA
Cover Design Patented: US 6,435,559 B2 • Printed in South Korea

Library of Congress Cataloging-in-Publication Data
Hibbard, Linda.
  Black and tan coonhound / by Linda Hibbard.
    p. cm.
  ISBN-13: 978-1-59378-393-8
  ISBN-10: 1-59378-393-0
  1. Black and tan coonhound. I. Title.
SF429.B56H53 2007
636.753'6--dc22
               2007022995

10 9 8 7 6 5 4 3 2 1

Photography by Isabelle Français
with additional photographs by:

Ashbey Photography, Carol Beuchat, Paulette Braun, Carolina Biological Supply, Kathy Corbett, Terri Dolbear, Earl Graham Studios, Carol Ann Johnson, Bill Jonas, Dr. Dennis Kunkel, Tam C. Nguyen, Phototake, Jean Claude Revy, Kit Rodwell and Jerry Vavra Photography.

Illustrations by Patricia Peters.

The publisher wishes to thank all of the owners whose dogs are illustrated in this book, including Edith S. Atchley, Dr. & Mrs. David Birdsall, Robert Browning, Jim & Kathy Corbett and Gene Hicks. Special thanks to Tanya Raab and the United Kennel Club for their invaluable assistance in the production of this book.

This hunt from the late 1960s yielded 117 coons. From left to right: Jim Adams with Midge and son; Robert Browning with Ch. Browning's Trooper; the Luttrell boys with Browning's Rambling Joe; Ed Foley with Hobo; and Harold Luttrell with Ch. Luttrell's Tiger.

BLACK AND TAN COONHOUND

The Black and Tan Coonhound is an American breed with ancient origins. Its history goes back to the European lines of the St. Hubert, Talbot, Bloodhound and other slow-trailing hounds that hunted in an independent manner.

The St. Hubert Hound is a descendent of the ancient hounds. It is known for being massively built and possessing an incredible scenting ability. The St. Hubert, like other strains of hound, was developed to perform jobs that were beneficial to their owners. As time passed, the Europeans went on to infuse the St. Hubert with lighter-built scenting hounds. The offspring proved to be better on the hunt, as they could run faster and did not tire as easily. Some of the hounds hunted in packs and lived in large groups while other strains tended to hunt independently. These early hounds were the foundation stock for the Bloodhound. Later, other strains of dog, such as the Foxhound, American cur and various shepherd types that worked on the farms, were crossbred to the early hounds. Such breeding was the beginning of the Black and Tan Coonhound.

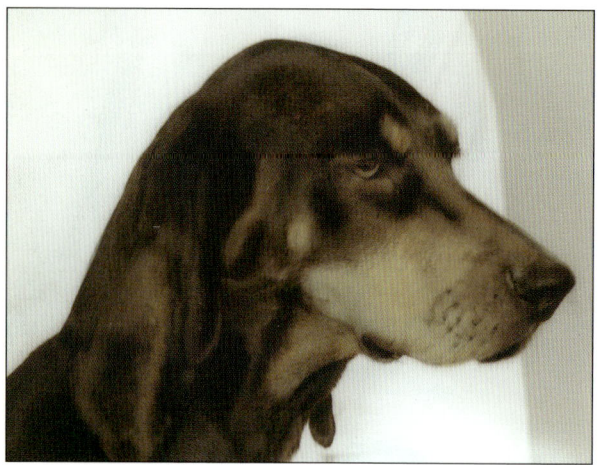

An early color photograph of Ch. Nite Ch. Browning's Mindy, one of the first UKC Dual Champion female Black and Tans, out of Ch. Rollridge Anna Belle.

Warren Sturtz is the owner of many UKC champions. Pictured on the right is Warren's grandfather, Arthur Sturtz, with Ole Rock. The identity of Arthur's hunting companion on the left is unknown.

The Black and Tan Coonhound is known for being a treeing hound. Before the development of the Coonhound in the American Colonies, it is doubtful if hounds were genetically inclined to tree their game. They did not run to the tree and place their legs on the trunk and give a full cry letting their owner know that the game had been located in the branches above. In England and France there were few animals that hid in the branches of trees. In the Colonies, however, there was an abundance of game, both large and small, that sought refuge in the trees, and this game, including bears, mountain lions, raccoons and gray foxes, could be treed by the dogs.

The Coonhound's ability to tree game is attributed to various infusions with strains of hounds that were brought to the Colonies from England and France. In order to understand the unique and special abilities of the Coonhound, it is necessary to go back in time and look at the history of the strains of hound that were imported to the new land and later infused together to produce this new type of hunting dog.

THE EARLY SCENTHOUNDS

Before the Christian era it was the Celtic people who were credited with breeding the earliest of the scenthounds. Dogs were not listed as pedigree or mongrel but were grouped and classified according to the type of job they performed. A dog's physical appearance had nothing to do with its value or desirability. A hound's value was based on its ability to do its job. The scenthounds that were owned by the Celtic people excelled in their ability to trail and made for good working hounds.

Selective breeding was done on the basis of picking the best dog

for the particular type of work to be done and breeding that dog to another of equal or superior quality. The large Celtic mastiff-like dog, although excellent in its scenting ability, was slow-moving and tired easily. People were in need of a dog faster on the chase and one that could keep up with its master as he hunted the rugged terrain. In order to produce such a dog, the mastiff type was crossbred with lighter-build scenthounds. The resulting offspring, although retaining the long floppy ears of the heavier dog, acquired the body type of the lighter-build hounds and was able to hunt with less effort and more endurance. One of the better-known hybrids that proved to be a superior scenting dog was the St. Hubert.

BREED DEVELOPMENT

It was in the Belgium monastery of St. Hubert's during the seventh century that the monks began producing dogs that, when bred to other members of the breed, would look identical and continue breeding true generation after generation. Such an accomplishment would be the beginning of

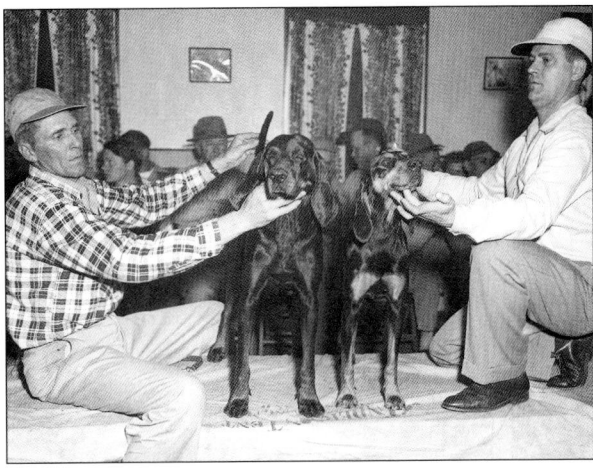

Clark Chaney and Ch. Chaney's Black George (LEFT) with Robert Browning and Ch. Rollridge Anna Bell; George and Anna Bell produced Ch. Nite Ch. Browning's Mindy, one of the first UKC bench and Nite Champions.

dogs being grouped and classified as pure-bred. The monks started their breeding program with a generalized Celtic type of hound from Gaul, France. The St. Hubert Hound not only was breeding true but also retained its excellent scenting ability. This new breed of dog was of medium size and build and possessed a large head and thick bones—its coloring was black and tan. This dog had a melodic voice and superior scenting ability and hunted in a slow manner. Word quickly spread about the dog and before long the St. Hubert was known throughout Europe. It was used in the foundation stock for many of the scenting type of hunting dogs, including the Talbot Hound and the modern-day Bloodhound.

Selective breeding produced hounds that were able to hunt in packs. The dogs were good-natured, sociable and proved to be

WHAT'S IN A NAME?

The original name of the breed was the American Black and Tan Fox and Coonhound. This is the name the United Kennel Club gave the breed when it was first recognized in 1900.

The Brownings with Gr. Ch. "PR" Browning's Black Beauty, the first to earn the National Grand Show Championship, at Autumn Oaks in 1977.

of excellent scenting ability. Many of the physical and psychological traits of the St. Hubert Hounds were passed onto the Bloodhound and the Black and Tan Coonhound. As its popularity grew the St. Hubert's genetics were infused into the stock of many of the scenting hounds.

THE BLOODHOUND AND ITS EFFECT

The Black and Tan Coonhound is a direct descendent of the Bloodhound, Talbot and various strains of the early Foxhounds. It was William the Conqueror who brought Bloodhounds to England in 1066. The Bloodhound has always been associated with royalty. They were referred to as the "blooded hounds" and were considered noble and pure. It was the custom of English royalty to give Bloodhounds as gifts to both royalty and nobility. It was also a

custom of the St. Hubert's Monastery to send a pair of their finest black and tan Bloodhounds to the king of France twice a year. In France the Bloodhound was mixed with other strains of hounds, including the Talbot Hound. As the popularity of the hound strains increased, the dogs quickly spread throughout Europe.

The Black and Tan Coonhound is a direct descendent of the Bloodhound.

Long before the Bloodhounds were used to track fugitives, noblemen used them as hunting partners. The Bloodhound was proficient at locating wild boar and deer that hid on the land. They would locate their quarry but not attack it, as the Bloodhound possessed a mild temper and was not bred for the purpose of attacking the game. Later the Bloodhound was used in Europe for tracking and locating lost people and fugitives. They possessed good senses of smell and never attacked the person whom they were pursuing. The Scots used the breed for tracking fugitives in the west of Scotland, and the English used the Bloodhound for tracking down sheep and cattle thieves and poachers. The Bloodhound was also referred to as the Sluthhound for obvious reasons, and it was even used in the search for the infamous Jack the Ripper.

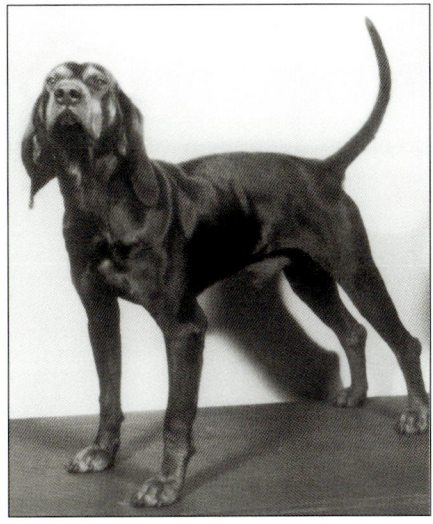

Owner Gene Hicks' Ch. Nite Ch. Gr. Ch. PR Hicks' Black Bandit earned his titles by the age of three.

HISTORY OF THE FOXHOUNDS
There is little doubt that the Bloodhound developed before the Foxhound. The English Foxhound was bred for the specific purpose of hunting fox, a sport dating back to the 13th century. The Foxhound is a scenthound with good endurance that hunts in packs. The early Foxhounds were developed from scenthounds that, when bred together, produced traits that made them excellent hunting dogs. They were well suited for following hunters over hundreds of miles of brush in weather that was less than mild and often extremely cold and rainy. Great care went into the development and refinement of the Foxhound.

Robert Brooke is credited with bringing the first Foxhounds to the Colonies in 1602. He arrived in America with Lord Baltimore and settled in Prince George

Like the American Foxhound pictured here, the Black and Tan Coonhound is descended from the Foxhounds brought to the early American Colonies.

Mary Lou and Robert Browning with Nite Ch. Browning's Rambling Joe, winner of the Nite Hunt at Black and Tan Days in 1966.

born and bred in the Colonies was termed an American Foxhound.

The American Foxhounds were of assorted varieties and divided into Southern or Pack Divisions. Some of the better-known strains were the Trigg, Goodman, Birdsong and Virginia Black and Tan. The Southern strains were quite numerous and, in addition, there were several small breeders who raised their own cold-trailing hounds. Merritt and Gossett are two of the well-known family names of the time. Many of the cold-nose strains were named for the area in which they developed, such as the Adirondacks, Catskills, White Mountains and Green Mountains. Both family named and geographically named strains were referred to as American Foxhounds.

As a result of the number of different strains, all bred for specific purposes, distinct charac-

County, Maryland. Most of the early Foxhounds can be traced back to his stock. It was after Brooke arrived that other wealthy people came to the Colonies and brought their best packs of Foxhounds with them. The Brooke strain was crossed with other strains of imported Foxhounds. The Coonhound and the American Foxhound are directly descended from the lines of Robert Brooke and other early pioneers who brought their Foxhounds to the Colonies.

Foxhounds, including the Virginia Foxhound and the English and American Foxhounds, were grouped together and referred to as American Foxhounds. Various new strains were constantly developing. The American strains differed from foreign strains, and a division of the two types took place. Any Foxhound that was

Harold Luttrell with Smokey, a son out of Ch. Nite Ch. Browning's Mindy.

teristics manifested themselves. Various strains of Foxhounds possessed different characteristics, such as voice tone, size and ear length.

The Vermont Foxhounds were more aggressive and were smaller in size and ear length. The Helderberg hounds were spotted hounds and had excessively long ears. The Adirondacks were white with lemon spots. All of theses strains had one thing in common, though: they were dogs that possessed pack instinct. The pack strains were rapidly outnumbering the solitary hunting hound found in the northern part of the country.

THE FORMATION OF THE BLACK AND TAN COONHOUND
The Black and Tan Coonhound, also referred to as the Cooner, developed in the regions of the Appalachian, Ozark, Blue Ridge and Smoky Mountains. It is an American breed made up of strains and breeds descended from both England and America.

The development of the Black and Tan Coonhound started a century before the American Revolution. Wealthy and titled Englishmen brought various types of hounds to the American Colonies. Over a period of time, the hounds were crossed with foxhounds native to the area and various strains of Curs and shepherd-type dogs. It was from these lines that the Coonhound

and the American Foxhound are directly descended.

When the Bloodhound arrived in America, it was primarily the people who were unable to afford expensive horses who used the breed. It was often the farmers who hunted with Bloodhounds on foot while the more affluent classes rode horseback while hunting their Foxhounds in packs. The Bloodhound was a dog of the common man, a good hunting partner that provided its owner with food for the table and skins that put money in its owner's pocket. It possessed good scenting ability and hunted in an independent manner, not of a pack type. It became the working man's dog, ideal for hunting and also protecting the farmers from local Indian attacks.

Bill Schenker with Dual Gr. Ch. Schenker's Black Jet, out of Dual Gr. Ch. Schenker's Black Smoky and Dual Ch. Logan's Black Bell.

Breeding was not based on fixed standards as it was in the old countries. Dogs were bred for assisting their owners in working for the necessities of life. The appearance of the dog or its ancestry was of no value to the farmers. It was during the 1800s that farmers found themselves in need of a hound that could be faster on the hunt, keep up with its owner and not tire as easily. It was crossbreeding to various foxhound strains that

DOG WORLD

The World's Largest All Breed Dog Magazine

MAY 1985 $2.50
                                           Canada: $3.00

Changing
scene at AKC?

The owner/vet
relationship

Socialize your
puppies early!

Special Report

Westminster
& Beverly
Hills: big
shows on
both coasts

CHAMPION ROCKYTOP WINNIE
THE POOH, Black and Tan Coon-
hound shown with Agent Davin
McAteer. Best of Breed at the AKC
Centennial Show. Proudly owned
by Rockytop Black and Tans, 1924
Stevens Dr., Huntsville, Alabama
(page 85)

produced offspring that were more aggressive, lighter in build and possessing more endurance on the hunt.

In the southern part of the United States, two distinct types of foxhound were present: those that possessed an interest in treeing game and those that were more inclined to chase the game. Breeders, more interested in developing a tree-minded hound, selected foxhounds with less interest in chasing and more interest in treeing game. This breeding was without a doubt the beginning of the Black and Tan Coonhound.

The evolution of the Black and Tan Coonhound can likely be traced to a pack of dogs owned by Colonel George Lawrence F. Birdsong, who was born in Georgia in 1821. From Birdsong's writings we find that his hounds came to Georgia from Virginia and were bred by Dr. Thomas Henry and his brother. It was Dr. Henry who had heard of a Dr. Buchanan from Sharpsburg, Maryland and the quality of his strain, and in 1842 he went to see Buchanan's stock. Dr. Buchanan offered Dr. Henry the best of his offspring; Dr. Henry accepted the offering and named the dogs Captain and Jim.

From correspondence between Colonel Birdsong and a Colonel

This is Gene Hicks with Grand Nite Ch. Hicks' Dynamite Dan.

Trigg, we find that Birdsong shipped three red and tan dogs, named George, Chase and Bee, to Colonel Trigg. The dogs went on

A multiple-Group winner, Ch. Traverse Hill Gypsy Woman, owned by Edith S. Atchley and William J. Gruner, was the number-three Black and Tan Coonhound in 1986.

to become the foundation stock of the famous Trigg strain, often referred to as the Full Cry strain. From this breeding the birth of the Black and Tan Coonhound was to take place.

In 1900 the American Black and Tan Coonhound became the first coonhound to gain recognition from the United Kennel Club (UKC). The UKC only registered strains of coonhounds with long ears, and dogs with shorter ears were not admitted to the registry. As time passed other breeders joined together with the intention of getting the Black and Tan Coonhound registered with the American Kennel Club (AKC).

AMERICAN KENNEL CLUB RECOGNITION

The American Kennel Club (AKC) first recognized the Black and Tan Coonhound in December of 1945, at which time it was admitted to the AKC Stud Book. The Black and Tan Coonhound is the first of the coonhound varieties to gain admittance into the AKC. The acceptance of the breed paved the way for the Black and Tan Coonhound to be

ROBERT BROWNING: A BREED'S CHAMPION

Although he can't receive credit as father of the Black and Tan Coonhound, Robert Browning surely is one of the most responsible for the breed's well-earned status among hunters and coonhound proponents throughout the US. Following the club's steady growth, Browning (pictured here in 1947 with his first Black and Tan, Browning's Dixie) was the catalyst for having the American Black and Tan Association (ABTA) become the first charter breed association of the United Kennel Club (UKC).

In addition to being a go-between for Dr. Edwin Gould, president of the UKC, and the ABTA, of which he would also serve as president, Browning was also involved in creating the Autumn Oaks competition as well as establishing the UKC Nite Hunt Honor Rules. Not only did Browning hunt his dogs successfully, he and his dogs also flourished in the show ring; he finished over 30 dogs as champions. Ch. "PR" Rollridge Anna Belle, who often took Best Female in Show, peeked Browning's interest in showing, while his Gr. Ch. "PR" Browning's Black Beauty won the first ever National Grand Show Championship.

shown in pure-bred dog shows sponsored by the AKC.

The Black and Tan that leads the registration list of the AKC is Grand Mere Big Rock Molly, who was owned by John C. Ellsworth and bred by John Evans of Big Rock, Illinois. Molly was born on March 12, 1936. The first champion to be recognized by the AKC was Grand Mere Lassie. The lines of the Grand Mere dogs are of interest in the history of the breed. They were carefully bred to produce show-quality Black and Tan Coonhounds. Orville O. Dunham of Niles, Michigan owned the line, and he is well recognized as being a pioneer in the development of show-stock Black and Tan Coonhounds. Some of his outstanding champions included Ch. Grand Mere, Grand Mere Wise Girel, Ch. Grand Mere Night Song, Ch. Grand Mere Wise Girel, Ch. Grand Mere Satin, Ch. My Buddy Grand Mere, Ch. Grand Mere His Majesty, Ch. Grand Mere Susan and Ch. Black Jack of Grand Mere.

Mignon Murray produced one of the most famous lines of Black and Tan Coonhounds. He is credited with the honor of breeding Ch. Karlena's Musical C Note, the first Black and Tan Coonhound to compete at Westminster and winner of Best of Breed in 1949. Ch. Karlena's Musical C Note produced 11 champions. For the following 20

Best of Breed at Westminster in 2002, this is Ch. Designer Southern Tradition, handled by Donald R. Powell II under judge John D. White Jr.

years it was either Ch. Karlena's Musical Ratter or Ch. Migone's Musical Junior, both C Note's prodigy and owned by Ann Clark, who won Best of Breed at the prestigious Westminster show.

Ch. Traverse Hill Flashdance, winning Best of Breed at the Harrisburg Kennel Club in 1988.

The Black and Tan Coonhound is a sturdy, rugged dog blessed with natural beauty, making it well suited for the show ring, as well as excellent skills on the hunt. Pictured is Ch. Wyeast Why Not, a Best in Show winner in the late 1980s.

CHARACTERISTICS OF THE

BLACK AND TAN COONHOUND

Above all, the Black and Tan Coonhound possesses a passion for hunting. The coldest nose hunter of the Hound Group, the Coonhound lives for the thrill of the hunt and the joy of being in nature. He possesses a drive to hunt at night, strictly by scent, and trees his game. When he is successful in locating the game, he lets out a full cry that signals his hunter. The Black and Tan has the nose, drive and stamina needed to hunt not only raccoon but also other large and small game, such as squirrel, fox, mountain lion and bear. The breed is more popular in the areas where he was originally developed, these being the mountainous areas of the Ozarks, Appalachians, Smokies and other regions of the southern portion of the United States.

It is not uncommon for a Coonhound to be a squirrel-hunting dog during the day and change into a raccoon hunter at night. The Black and Tan Coonhound, named for his ability to hunt the coon, was rarely bought for the sole purpose of hunting raccoon. He is a physically diversi-fied hunter, able to hunt over difficult terrain, in a tireless manner, in temperatures that range from extreme hot to extreme cold.

HUNTING CHARACTERISTICS
The hunting Coonhound are of two varieties: those that hunt in the manner and style of the straddler and those that hunt in the style of the drifter. Straddlers follow the ground scent track by track. They are better locators but bark constantly while hunting. Drifters follow the scent until it fades, then hold their heads up in search of a better scent. Drifters tree quicker and have a better handle on the air currents. The variation in style is attributed to the differences in strains within the breed.

Coonhounds not only are fine hunters but they also make wonderful companions and show dogs. Although the Coonhound has always been more popular as a hunter, some owners show their Black and Tan Coonhounds. Coonhounds of the show variety tend to be less aggressive and smaller in size and possess less hunting instinct.

TEMPERAMENT

The Black and Tan Coonhound is even-tempered, friendly and outgoing. He can be reserved but should never be shy or vicious. Most importantly he should never show aggression toward people or other dogs. The breed works well with other hounds and cooperates in the hunt.

The Black and Tan makes an excellent companion dog, as he is a pack animal and needs to be around people. He quickly bonds to his owner and is a loyal and devoted companion. The Black and Tan Coonhound is never a laid-back dog and has a high energy level, needing constant interaction with his owner. The Coonhound also makes a fine watchdog and needs no formal training, as his forbidding size and intense bark are intimidating to any stranger.

THE IDEAL OWNER

The Black and Tan Coonhound should be appropriately matched with his owner, as he is not a dog for everyone. His hunting needs limit the type of person who will do best as his owner. The Coonhound is first and foremost a hunting dog with an inborn instinct to tree his game. He does best with an owner that takes him on hunts and provides other outdoor activities suited to his hunting instinct and activity level.

Black and Tans have strong hunting instincts and will thrive in an environment that allows them the opportunity to really follow their noses.

The Coonhound should never be left off leash when in public, as he will wander, and possibly run, in search of game. The Black and Tan is an extremely fast runner and does best with an owner that is both active and athletic. Due to his active nature, the Coonhound should be in an environment that is conducive to his needs; he will adapt better to rural living than to city life.

The Coonhound, being a pack animal, needs both the constant company and attention of his owner. If left alone for extended periods of time, he will become bored, and when boredom sets in he will find something to occupy his time. If left inside the house he will often get into the garbage or chew the furniture. Should he be outside too long and boredom overtakes him, he could turn into an escape artist—jumping fences or digging holes in the yard. Invisible fences will not work for the Coonhound, as he has a high tolerance for pain. He is a dog inclined to bark for hours at a time in to order to get the desired attention and affection he seeks.

The Black and Tan is a great companion for older children, as he enjoys being part of their adventurous world, especially when they provide him with the opportunity to run and play in the woods. Being a strong and powerful dog, he should not have unsupervised interaction with younger children, especially infants and toddlers, as he could accidentally hurt them. The Black and Tan has a natural instinct to chase cats because he views them as his game, so it is advised that Coonhound owners not own indoor cats.

The present Coonhound has retained his loud bawl. His barking traits are inborn and cannot be changed with behavior modification. Therefore it is recommended that owners of Black and Tans not live in cities or other heavily populated areas. The breed should not be kept in apartments or confined to other small quarters, as he will become relatively inactive. Coonhounds need to be in large yards with proper fencing, as they can escape to go on the prowl in search of game. The Cooner needs an owner who can provide lots of attention and companionship. Anyone who works long hours or is away from home for extended periods of time will have trouble with this breed.

The Coonhound has a reputation for being hard to train in areas of obedience. He needs to be in training classes from puppyhood to his senior years. Conventional training tends to be difficult, as the Coonhound is stubborn and strong willed. He needs to be with an owner who will constantly provide firm

The Black and Tan Coonhound is an affectionate and intelligent dog that will be an excellent companion for the right owner.

HEALTH ISSUES OF THE BLACK AND TAN COONHOUND

The Black and Tan Coonhound is a healthy and hardy dog. He has few known genetic problems, but, like all dogs, there are certain inherited conditions that are passed from generation to generation. Perspective Coonhound owners should be aware of both serious and minor health problems that exist in the breed.

PROGRESSIVE RETINAL ATROPHY

Progressive retinal atrophy (PRA) is a serious condition that affects a dog's eyesight, ultimately resulting in blindness. There is no known treatment for the condition. Normally it is only males that are affected with the defective gene that causes this condition. Females can be carriers, and all mothers of the affected males will be carriers as well as all daughters of affected males.

Progressive retinal atrophy is a disorder that affects the rods and cones of the retinal photoreceptors. As a general rule the rods will be damaged first, causing an inability for the dog to see at night. Night blindness is a term often used to describe the first stage of this disorder. As the condition progresses the cones become damaged resulting in total loss of eyesight. The condition, however, is not painful. Few symptoms normally associated with eye disorders,

guidance and control. Any type of physical punishment will not work with this breed, as physical force will result in a frightened and shy Coonhound. A trusting bond needs to develop between the dog and his owner.

There are two distinct types of Black and Tan Coonhounds: the show dog and the hunting dog. Show dogs are usually bred smaller in size, and they possess less aggressive tendencies. They are also less work-oriented and make better pets. The breed, however, has always been more popular for hunting than showing.

such as red eyes, squinting and blinking, are present. Symptoms are subtle and generally noticed when the dog's eyes have a distinctive shine in appearance. The shine indicates the eyes are not able to dilate as they should and a failed attempt to take in more light has resulted. The lens of the eye will eventually begin to look opaque, which means that a cloud has formed over the eye.

Genetic testing is now available to determine if your Coonhound has the defective gene. The testing is inexpensive and painless and is performed at the veterinarian's office. It involves only drawing blood from the dog, which is then sent to the laboratory for testing. Dogs testing positive should not be used for breeding.

HIP DYSPLASIA

Hip dysplasia is a serious heredi-tary condition that affects the dog's hip joints. Hip dysplasia occurs when the head of the femur bone does not fit properly into the socket. When the condition is present it causes the joints to become inflamed, which produces both pain and weakness, especially when the dog exercises. As the abnormality progresses, the hips continue to deteriorate and arthritis results. There are varying degrees of canine hip dyslplasia, ranging from mild cases to those that result in crippling arthritis.

Hip dysplasia is not a disease of old age. It is a condition that develops while the puppy is still growing and developing. Some dogs exhibit traits of the disease at as early as four months of age. Other dogs do not show signs of the condition until they are grown or well into their senior years.

The first signs of hip dysplasia in a puppy is a gait that appears to be abnormal, such as running with both legs nearly together, giving the appearance of running like a rabbit. In mature or older dogs the first signs of the problem may appear suddenly when they are reluctant to run and jump or they hesitate going up and down stairs.

Should you have any question about the possibility of your dog having hip dysplasia, it is a good idea to have your dog examined by a veterinarian in order to rule out such a problem. The veteri-narian will examine your Coonhound to make sure the hip joint has a proper range of motion and that the joint, when extended, is in the proper range. The doctor will also listen for the typical sound of a click that indicates the hip is popping out of the joint and that there is cartilage loss.

Treatment is available for hip dysplasia. If a mild condition exists, weight should be monitored so that additional stress is not put on the affected joints. Exercise needs to be kept to a moderate amount, which can present a problem for the Coonhound, as he is used to vigorous exercise. Anti-inflammatory drugs can reduce the pain and keep the inflammation to a minimum. If the condition worsens surgical treatment is also an option. Medical procedures are available for both young and old Coonhounds.

Have your Coonhound screened for hip dysplasia and other genetic disorders. This can be done by the Orthopedic Foundation for Animals (OFA), a non-profit organization that provides radiographic evaluation, database maintenance and breeding advice to reduce the incidence of canine hip dysplasia. Also, take precautions before selecting your new Coonhound puppy that the breeder of the litter has had both the sire and dam's hips tested by the OFA. Do not purchase a puppy whose parents achieve scores of anything less than Good or Excellent. If the breeder has not had the parents OFA tested for hip dysplasia, do not purchase the puppy; you also should look for a new breeder as well.

ECTROPION

Black and Tan Coonhounds are prone to developing a disorder known as ectropion, a genetically inherited condition resulting in the sagging or rolling out of the eyelids. The defective conformation produces excessive exposure of the eye that can cause irritation and infection.

Ectropion is thought to be associated with several genes affecting the way the skin covers the head and face of the Coonhound. When predisposed to ectropion, irritants to the eye can cause inflammation both to the eyelids and the membrane of the eye. The eyes of the Coonhound can become dry as they produce less moisture that is necessary for the cleaning of the cornea.

Symptoms of ectropion are red eyes and a discharge coming from one or both eyes. The eyelids tend to look as if they are sagging in an exaggerated manner, and the production of liquid in the eyes is greatly reduced. Mild cases of the condition do not require any formal treatment. It is only when the problem becomes chronic that surgery should be considered. The surgical procedure is not extensive and involves removing a small section of tissue from the eyelid margin. Coonhounds that require surgery for ectropion are prohibited from being exhibited in the show ring. Ectropion results from breeding to produce desired traits such as heavy facial folds. In order to lessen the condition, breeding specimens should have less-exaggerated facial features.

Good breeders strive to keep their line of dogs healthy by regularly screening for genetic disorders.

BLACK AND TAN COONHOUND

The breed standard serves as a blueprint of the ideal member of that breed, guiding how dogs are judged in shows and how breeders plan their breeding programs.

The Black and Tan Coonhound is a working dog. He is a skillful hunter who hunts almost entirely by scent and trees his game. He is a cold-nose hunter and is happiest when he is in the country hunting game. He is a large and powerful dog with an elegant graceful appearance, holding his head high with an air of elegance. He moves with even, flowing motions. As his name implies he is black and tan in color, the coloring a velvety jet black with rich tan trim and markings. Over both eyes are tan dots, often referred to as "pumpkin seeds."

The breed standard is a detailed description of the physical traits and desired temperament of the ideal Black and Tan Coonhound. There is no Black and Tan Coonhound that can match the standard entirely, as the standard is a written description of what the perfect dog should look and act like. The perfect dog does not exist and, therefore, the breed is judged individually on traits that come closest to what is written in the standard.

Faults within the standards are listed as both minor and major. Obviously, dogs displaying minor faults are penalized less severely than dogs possessing major faults. Extreme faults are listed as disqualifications and prevent the dog from being shown.

The United Kennel Club (UKC) and American Kennel Club (AKC) are major registries that recognize the Black and Tan Coonhound. Both registries have their own breed standard, which is written by officially recognized parent clubs. The UKC accepted the Black and Tan Coonhound in 1900, while the American Kennel

Club recognized the breed in December 1945. The American Black and Tan Coonhound Club, which is the parent breed club representing the AKC, was organized in the 1970s. The first specialty show took place on November 24, 1978, and the American Black and Tan Coonhound Club has continued to hold specialty shows once a year under the direction of the American Kennel Club.

There are very few differences between the UKC and AKC standards; perhaps the most noticeable difference is in accepted heights of both the males and females. The United Kennel Club's standard calls for the height of males to be 23 to 27 inches at the shoulder and the height of females to be 21 to 26 inches at the shoulder. The American Kennel Club's standard requires males to be 25 inches to 27 inches at the shoulder and females to be 23 inches to 25 inches at the shoulder. The other noticeable difference between the two standards is that the American Kennel Club's standard is written in more detail.

Standards are desirable as they unify different strains and varieties into one breed type, consistently producing offspring that look alike. Breed standards also help to encourage an international breed type resulting in a universal conformation of the breed.

THE AKC STANDARD FOR THE BLACK AND TAN COONHOUND

General Appearance: The Black and Tan Coonhound is first and fundamentally a working dog, a trail and tree hound, capable of withstanding the rigors of winter, the heat of summer, and the

difficult terrain over which he is called upon to work. Used principally for trailing and treeing raccoon, the Black and Tan Coonhound runs his game entirely by scent. The characteristics and courage of the Coonhound also make him proficient on the hunt for deer, bear, mountain lion and other big game. Judges are asked by the club sponsoring the breed to place great emphasis upon these facts when evaluating the merits of the dog. The general impression is that of power, agility and alertness. He immediately impresses one with his ability to cover the ground with powerful rhythmic strides.

Size, Proportion, Substance: *Size* measured at the shoulder—Males 25 to 27 inches; females 23 to 25 inches. Oversized dogs should not be penalized when general soundness and proportion are in favor. Penalize undersize. *Proportion*—Measured from the point of shoulder to the buttocks and from withers to ground the length of body is equal to or slightly greater than the height of the dog at the withers. Height is in proportion to general conformation so that dog appears neither leggy nor close to the ground. *Substance*—Considering their job as a hunting dog, the individual should exhibit moderate bone and good muscle tone. Males are heavier in bone and muscle tone than females.

Head: The head is cleanly modeled. From the back of the skull to the nose the head measures from 9 to 10 inches in males and from 8 to 9 inches in females. *Expression* is alert, friendly and eager. The skin is devoid of folds. Nostrils well open and always black. The flews are well developed with typical hound appearance. Penalize excessive wrinkles. *Eyes* are from hazel to dark brown in color, almost round and not deeply set. Penalize yellow or light eyes. *Ears* are low set and well back. They hang in graceful folds, giving the dog a majestic appearance. In length they extend naturally well beyond the tip of the nose and are set at eye level or lower. Penalize ears that do not reach the tip of the nose and are set too high on the head. *Skull* tends toward oval outline. Medium stop occurring midway between occiput bone and nose. Viewed from profile the line of the skull is on a practically parallel plane to the foreface or muzzle. *Teeth* fit evenly with scissors bite. Penalize excessive deviation from scissors bite.

Neck, Topline, Body: The neck is muscular, sloping, medium length. The skin is devoid of excess dewlap. The back is level,

PURCHASING A PROSPECTIVE SHOW-QUALITY COONHOUND
When buying a prospective show puppy, it is imperative you be familiar with the breed standard. The standard is a written description of what the ideal member of the breed should look like. Dogs that mature into specimens that come close to the standard are referred to as "show quality." Dogs that fall short of the written standard are considered "pet quality." A good breeder should assist you with choosing a puppy that appears to have the traits that are required by the standard.

Black and Tan Coonhound head study of correct type.

hock long and sinewy, hock to pad short and strong. Stifles and hocks well bent and not inclining either in or out. When standing on a level surface, the hind feet are set back from under the body and the leg from pad to hock is at right angles to the ground. *Fault*—Rear dewclaws.

Coat: The coat is short but dense to withstand rough going.

Color: As the name implies, the color is coal black with rich tan markings above eyes, on sides of muzzle, chest, legs and breeching, with black pencil markings on toes. Penalize lack of rich tan markings, excessive areas of tan markings, excessive black coloration. *Faults*—White on chest or other parts of body is highly undesirable, and a solid patch of white which extends more than one inch in any direction is a disqualification.

powerful and strong. The dog possesses full, round, well sprung ribs, avoiding flatsidedness. Chest reaches at least to the elbows. The *tail* is strong, with base slightly below level of backline, carried free and when in action at approximately right angle to back.

Forequarters: Powerfully constructed shoulders. The forelegs are straight, with elbows turning neither in nor out; pasterns strong and erect. *Feet* are compact, with well knuckled, strongly arched toes and thick, strong pads. Penalize flat or splayed feet.

Hindquarters: Quarters are well boned and muscled. From hip to

Gait: When viewed from the side, the stride of the Black and Tan Coonhound is easy and graceful with plenty of reach in front and drive behind. When viewed from the front the forelegs, which are in line with the width of the body, move forward in an effortless manner, but never cross. Viewed from the rear the hocks follow on a line with the forelegs, being neither too widely nor too closely spaced, and as the speed of the trot increases the feet tend to converge toward a center line or single track indicating soundness, balance and stamina. When in action, his head and tail carriage is proud and alert; the topline remains level.

Temperament: Even temperament, outgoing and friendly. As a working scent hound, must be able to work in close contact with other hounds. Some may be reserved but never shy or vicious. Aggression toward people or other dogs is most undesirable.

Note—Inasmuch as this is a hunting breed, scars from honorable wounds shall not be considered faults.

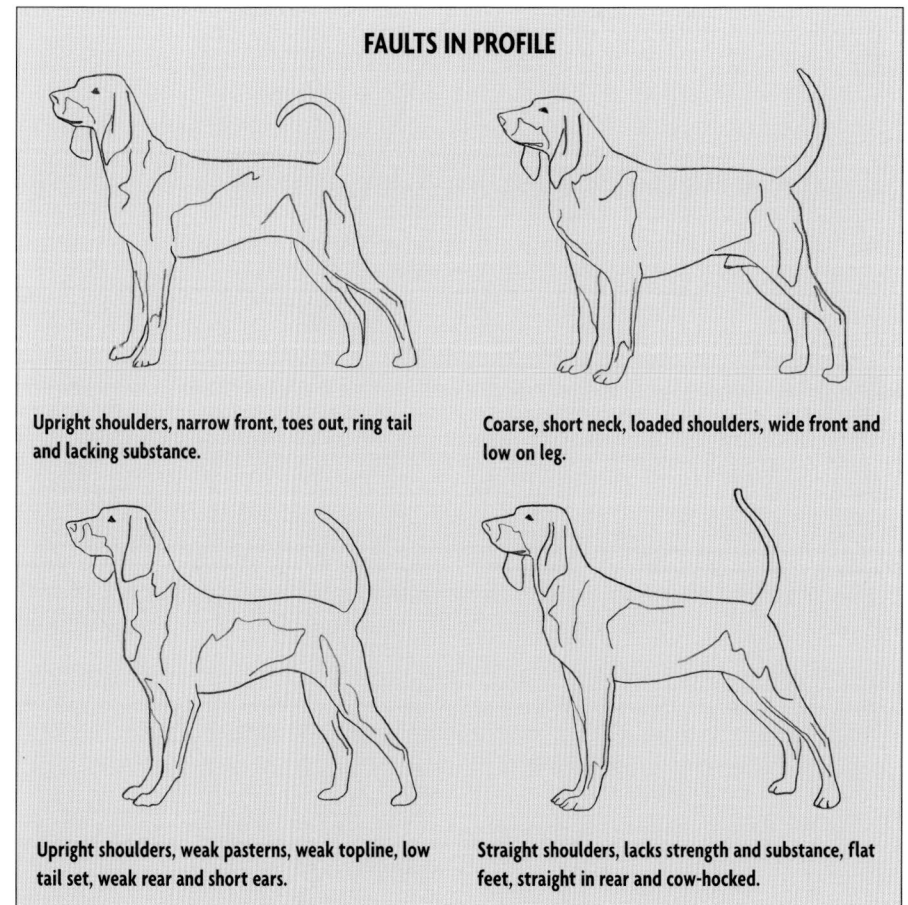

FAULTS IN PROFILE

Upright shoulders, narrow front, toes out, ring tail and lacking substance.

Coarse, short neck, loaded shoulders, wide front and low on leg.

Upright shoulders, weak pasterns, weak topline, low tail set, weak rear and short ears.

Straight shoulders, lacks strength and substance, flat feet, straight in rear and cow-hocked.

Disqualifications: A solid patch of white which extends more than one inch in any direction.

Approved December 11, 1990
Effective January 30, 1991

THE UKC STANDARD FOR THE AMERICAN BLACK AND TAN COONHOUND

HISTORY OF THE AMERICAN BLACK & TAN COONHOUND

The Black & Tan is one of many tracking breeds that was developed in the south of the United States. The breed can trace its immediate ancestry to the American Foxhound and the Virginia Foxhound of colonial days, with probably the introduction of some Bloodhound stock. This latter would explain not only the coloration of the Black & Tan, but its tendency toward being larger-boned than other breeds, its long ears, and its famous cold nose.

The American Black & Tan can probably be traced to the English Foxhounds, and before that to the Talbot Hounds and St. Hubert hounds of France. These hounds were first brought to England following the Norman invasion in the 11th century.

The American Black & Tan was the first coonhound breed to be admitted into registry with UKC. When they were first registered in 1900, and for several years after that, they were registered as American Black & Tan Fox & Coonhounds.

HEAD AND NECK
Head: Carried well up, very slightly domed and broad between the ears, never narrow. Neck not too thick, nor too long, but graceful and strong; minimum of dewlap.

Teeth: Scissors bite preferred, even bite acceptable.

Eyes: Prominent, hound-like, pleading expression. Dark brown or black, not lighter than hazel. Eyelids firm and close (no drooping).

Ears: Set medium low, well attached to head and devoid of erectile power, should reach approximately to end of nose when drawn out. Should hang

SCALE OF POINTS:

Head	10
Neck	5
Shoulders	10
Chest and Ribs	10
Back and Loins	15
Hindquarters	10
Elbows	5
Legs and Feet	20
Coat and Color	5
Stern	5
General Makeup	5
Total	**100**

gracefully, inside part tipping toward muzzle, should not be too pointed at tip, slightly oval, soft and velvety, hanging in a roll when head is raised.

Muzzle: Well-balanced with the other features of the head, medium square, with flews sufficient to give square appearance. Nostril large, open; black in color, never butterfly or pink.

SHOULDERS
Muscular and sloping; indicating speed and strength.

CHEST
Deep, moderately wide, showing large lung space.

BACK
Short and slightly arched, well-muscled and strong. This is one important part of this breed. A good rule to breed to is the same distance from root of tail to shoulder as height at shoulder.

HIPS
Smooth, round, proportionately wide, flanks gracefully arched, muscular at the loins, tail heavy, strong at root tapering there, rather long without brush, carried free, well-up, saber like.

LEGS
Front: Straight, smooth forearms, muscular, straight at knees, perfectly in line with upper leg.

Hind: Strong and muscular above hock. Slightly bent at hock and stifle, not cow hocked, free of dewclaws.

FEET
Tight and well padded. Toes short to medium and close knit. Neither cat-footed nor splay-footed. Foot to be proportionate to the size of the body.

COLOR AND COAT
Smooth haired, fine, glossy, but thick enough for protection. Predominantly deep, rich black, with tan trim covering not more than 10–15 percent of body. Small pumpkin seed over eyes. A little white on breast is not a fault, but no white elsewhere.

HEIGHT
Slightly more at shoulders than at hips. *Males:* 23 to 27 inches. *Females:* 21 to 26 inches.

WEIGHT
Males: 50 to 75 pounds. *Females:* 40 to 65 pounds. Dogs being shown slightly under weight due to hunting will not be penalized. This is a working breed and should appear as such.

CHARACTERISTICS OF THIS BREED
Active, fast, bright, kind, confident, courageous, with open trailing and treeing instinct and ability.

BLACK AND TAN COONHOUND

CHOOSING YOUR PUPPY

Choosing your Black and Tan Coonhound is a project that should not be taken lightly, and you should never make an impulsive decision in purchasing a Coonhound puppy or any other dog. Take ample time to study and acquaint yourself with the needs and temperament of this breed. Make sure that you will be able to provide a suitable home for the puppy once it has matured.

If you have decided that the Black and Tan Coonhound is the right breed for you then evaluate what you want to use your new puppy for. Are you interested in using your Coonhound for hunting, showing or simply as a companion dog? After you have made this decision it is now time to locate a breeder. Reputable breeders of pure-bred dogs will be registered with local breed clubs, hunt clubs or dog registries. Many of the hunting dog breeders register their dogs with the United Kennel Club and the American Kennel Club and can be located through the club's respective website. Registries can be located on the Internet and will send you addresses and phone numbers of breeders in your area. It is advisable, if geographically feasible, to go and see the litter you intend to purchase your puppy from. When evaluating a kennel, make sure the premises are clean and the number of dogs present is not excessive. Should you be purchasing a puppy over the Internet, proceed with caution and make sure the breeder is a reputable one.

When visiting the litter, do not hesitate to ask questions. If you are looking for a puppy that you will use for a certain purpose, such as hunting or conformation, make sure the breeder uses his dogs for such purposes. Visit with the parents of the litter and make

Observe the puppy's interaction with new people. He should be affectionate and friendly.

sure they are of a quality that you desire (sometimes the sire will not belong to the breeder, but the dam should be present). If you are looking for a hunting dog ask the breeder if you could accompany him on a short hunt with the sire or the dam. Quality breeders are more than willing to answer questions and enjoy sharing information about the quality of their dogs and any merits or awards they have garnered. When a breeder is evasive or put off by sensible questions, he should be avoided.

Should you be interested in purchasing a prospective show dog, be familiar with the breed's

SIGNS OF A HEALTHY PUPPY

Healthy puppies are robust little fellows who are alert and active, sporting shiny coats and supple skin. They should not appear lethargic, bloated or pot-bellied, nor should they have flaky skin or runny or crusted eyes or noses. Their stools should be firm and well formed, with no evidence of blood or mucus.

standard. Look for a litter of puppies that has been bred for show purposes, and ask the breeder about his lines. Also ask to look at the pedigrees to verify these lines. Check to see how many champions the sire and the dam of the litter have produced. If tho parents hold championship titles, chances are the offspring will have a greater likelihood of becoming a quality show dog. Remember that it is impossible to predict what a puppy will grow into, but by selecting a good breeder and studying the lines of the offspring you will have a better chance of getting the dog that will suit your intended purpose. A knowledgeable breeder will also be able to assist you in choosing a puppy that exhibits the traits you desire. No reputable breeder will guarantee that one of his puppies will become a proven hunter or a champion in the show ring. Such a

A puppy needs to remain with the breeder for a certain period of time so he can learn important life lessons from his mom. If the dam is not on the premises, continue your puppy search elsewhere.

Puppies nurse from their dam during their early weeks of life.

statement is not taking into consideration factors that could affect the dog's chances for showing or hunting.

Reputable breeders should, however, provide buyers with a written health guarantee stating that the puppy should be free from contagious illness for a reasonable period of time. Also breeders are often willing to stand behind their puppies for inherited conditions that would prevent the use of the dog for the purpose for which it was purchased. Guarantees for inherited conditions should not be for an unreasonably short period of time since many

inherited conditions do not present themselves early in a dog's life. If a breeder refuses to provide you with a written health guarantee, it is best to look for a puppy elsewhere.

WHAT TO LOOK FOR
When selecting a puppy to be used as a treeing hound, attempt to pick the pup that demonstrates the best qualities as a hunting type. The three major attributes that make for a good hunter are instinct, temperament and intelligence. Look for these traits in the pup.

Spend some time paying attention to how the puppies

A SHOW PUPPY

If you plan to show your puppy, you must first deal with a reputable breeder who shows his dogs and has had some success in the conformation ring. The puppy's pedigree should include one or more champions in the first and second generation. You should be familiar with the breed and breed standard so you can know what qualities to look for in your puppy. The breeder's observations and recommendations also are invaluable aids in selecting your future champion. If you consider an older puppy, be sure that the puppy has been properly socialized with people and not isolated in a kennel without substantial daily human contact.

interact with their siblings. A pup that dominates his siblings will grow up to be dominant and this type of personality can cause trouble. Also take notice of the puppy that hangs back, cowering in the corner. This pup is overly shy and will not make for a good hunting partner.

Take the remaining pups aside and see how they tend to react to you. Choose the pup that follows you for the longest amount of time. He is the one that is showing traits of intelligence, good temperament and nose.

MALE OR FEMALE?

The choice of a male or female is largely a matter of personal preference. There are advantages and disadvantages to both sexes. If you are interested in breeding you definitely want a female. Should you wish to show your dog, either male or female will be appropriate. It should be taken into consideration that the female will come into season twice a year.

For serious hunters a male may be preferable, as a dog will be larger and have a stronger bawl. The female, however, does not possess as strong an instinct to roam as does the male and this is an advantage.

Puppies will learn some rules of interaction from other puppies, but it will be up to you to continue this education once he's in your home.

For companionship purposes either a male or female will make a fine companion. Dogs that are not purchased for the intent of showing or breeding should be fixed.

YOUR BLACK AND TAN COONHOUND SHOPPING LIST

Just as expectant parents prepare a nursery for their baby, so should you ready your home for the arrival of your Black and Tan Coonhound pup. If you have the necessary puppy supplies purchased and in place before he comes home, it will ease the puppy's transition from the warmth and familiarity of his mom and littermates to the brand-new environment of his new home and human family. You will be too busy to stock up and prepare your house after your pup comes home, that's for sure. Imagine how a pup must feel upon being transported to a strange new place. It's up to you to comfort him and to let your little pup know that he is going to be happy with you.

FOOD AND WATER BOWLS

Your puppy will need separate bowls for his food and water. Stainless steel pans are generally preferred over plastic bowls since they sterilize better and pups are less inclined to chew on the metal. Heavy-duty ceramic bowls are popular, but consider how often you will have to pick up those heavy bowls. Buy adult-sized pans, as your puppy will grow into them before you know it.

THE DOG CRATE

If you think that crates are tools of punishment and confinement for when a dog has misbehaved, think again. Most breeders and almost all trainers recommend a crate as the preferred house-training aid as well as for all-around puppy training and safety. Because dogs are natural den creatures that prefer cave-like environments, the benefits of crate use are many. The crate provides the puppy with his very own "safe house," a cozy place

Stainless steel food and water bowls are the best for puppies, as they are less inclined to chew them.

to sleep, take a break or seek comfort with a favorite toy; a travel aid to house your dog when on the road, at motels or at the vet's office; a training aid to help teach your puppy proper toileting habits; and a place of solitude when non-dog people happen to drop by and don't want a lively puppy—or even a well-behaved adult dog—saying hello or begging for attention.

Crates come in several types, although the wire crate and the fiberglass airline-type crate are the most popular. Both are safe and your puppy will adjust to either one, so the choice is up to you. The wire crates offer better visibility for the pup as well as better ventilation. Many of the wire crates easily fold into suit-case-size carriers. The fiberglass crates, similar to those used by the airlines for animal transport, are sturdier and more den-like.

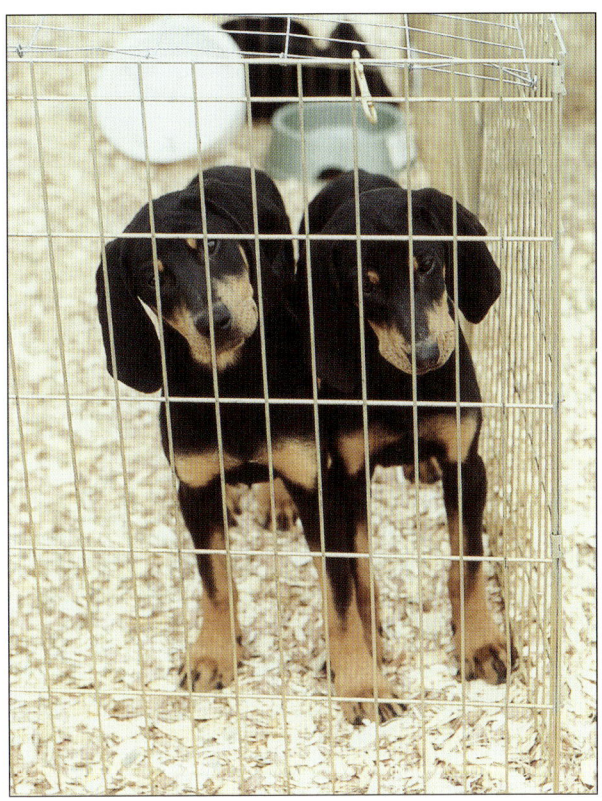

However, the fiberglass crates do not fold down and are less ventilated than a wire crate, which can be problematic in hot weather. Some of the newer crates are made of heavy plastic mesh; they are very lightweight and fold up into slim-line suit-cases. However, a mesh crate might not be suitable for a pup with manic chewing habits.

Don't bother with a puppy-sized crate. Although your Black and Tan Coonhound will be a little fellow when you bring him

Confinement is a big part of a puppy's growing up. This is first experienced at the breeder's home.

Bearing in mind that puppies grow at varying rates (even from the same litter), choose your Black and Tan puppy's toys and bedding wisely.

home, he will grow up in the blink of an eye and your puppy crate will be useless. Purchase a crate that will accommodate an adult Black and Tan Coonhound. He will stand about 25 to 27 inches when full grown, so a medium- to large-sized crate will fit him nicely.

BEDDING AND CRATE PADS
Your puppy will enjoy some type of soft bedding in his "room" (the crate), something he can snuggle into to feel cozy and secure. Old towels or blankets are good choices for a young pup, since he may (and probably will) have a toileting accident or two in the crate or decide to chew on the bedding material. Once he is fully trained and out of the early chewing stage, you can replace the puppy bedding with a perma-nent crate pad if you prefer. Crate pads and other dog beds run the gamut from inexpensive to high-end doggie-designer styles, but don't splurge on the good stuff until you are sure that your puppy is reliable and won't tear it up or make a mess on it.

PUPPY TOYS
Just as infants and older children require objects to stimulate their minds and bodies, puppies need toys to entertain their curious brains, wiggly paws and achy teeth. A fun array of safe doggie toys will help satisfy your puppy's chewing instincts and distract him from gnawing on the leg of your antique chair or your new leather sofa. Most puppy toys are cute and look as if they would be a lot of fun, but not all are necessarily safe or good for your puppy, so use caution when you go puppy-toy shopping.

CRATE EXPECTATIONS
To make the crate more inviting to your puppy, you can offer his first meal or two inside the crate, always keeping the crate door open so that he does not feel confined. Keep a favorite toy or two in the crate for him to play with while inside. You can also cover the crate at night with a lightweight sheet to make it more den-like and remove the stimuli of household activity. Never put him into his crate as punishment or as you are scolding him, since he will then associate his crate with negative situations and avoid going there.

Although Black and Tan Coonhounds are not known to be voracious chewers like many other dogs, they still love to chew. The best "chewcifiers" are nylon and hard rubber bones, which are safe to gnaw on and come in sizes appropriate for all age groups and breeds. Be especially careful of natural bones, which can splinter or develop dangerous sharp edges; pups can easily swallow or choke on those bone splinters. Veterinarians often tell of surgical nightmares involving bits of splintered bone, because in addition to the danger of choking, the sharp pieces can damage the intestinal tract.

Similarly, rawhide chews, while a favorite of most dogs and puppies, can be equally dangerous. Pieces of rawhide are easily swallowed after they got soft and gummy from chewing, and dogs have been known to choke on pieces of ingested rawhide. Rawhide chews should be offered only when you can supervise the puppy.

Soft woolly toys are special puppy favorites. They come in a wide variety of cute shapes and sizes; some look like little stuffed animals. Puppies love to shake them up and toss them about or simply carry them around. Be careful of fuzzy toys that have button eyes or noses that your pup could chew off and swallow, and make sure that he does not

TOYS 'R SAFE

The vast array of tantalizing puppy toys is staggering. Stroll through any pet shop or pet-supply outlet and you will see that the choices can be overwhelming. However, not all dog toys are safe or sensible. Most very young puppies enjoy soft woolly toys that they can snuggle with and carry around. (You know they have outgrown them when they shred them up!) Avoid toys that have buttons, tabs or other enhancements that can be chewed off and swallowed. Soft toys that squeak are fun, but make sure your puppy does not disembowel the toy and remove (and swallow) the squeaker. Toys that rattle or make noise can excite a puppy, but they present the same danger as the squeaky kind and so require supervision. Hard rubber toys that bounce can also entertain a pup, but make sure that the toy is too big for your pup to swallow.

TOXIC PLANTS

Plants are natural puppy magnets, but many can be harmful, even fatal, if ingested by a puppy or adult dog. Scout your yard and home interior and remove any plants, bushes or flowers that could be even mildly dangerous. It could save your puppy's life. You can obtain a complete list of toxic plants from your veterinarian, at the public library or by looking online.

disembowel a squeaky toy to remove the squeaker! Braided rope toys are similar in that they are fun to chew and toss around, but they shred easily and the strings are easy to swallow. The strings are not digestible and, if the puppy doesn't pass them in his stool, he could end up at the vet's office. As with rawhides,

your puppy should be closely monitored with rope toys.

If you believe that your pup has ingested a piece of one of his toys, check his stools for the next couple of days to see if he passes the item when he defecates. At the same time, also watch for signs of intestinal distress. A call to your veterinarian might be in order to get his advice and be on the safe side.

An all-time favorite toy for puppies (young and old!) is the empty gallon milk jug. Hard plastic juice containers—46 ounces or more—are also excellent. Such containers make lots of noise when they are batted about, and puppies go crazy with delight as they play with them. However, they don't often last very long, so be sure to remove and replace them when they get chewed up.

A word of caution about homemade toys: be careful with your choices of non-traditional play objects. Never use old shoes or socks, since a puppy cannot distinguish between the old ones on which he's allowed to chew and the new ones in your closet that are strictly off limits. That principle applies to anything that resembles something that you don't want your puppy to chew.

COLLARS

A lightweight nylon collar is the best choice for a very young pup. Quick-click collars are easy to put on and remove, and they can be adjusted as the puppy grows. Introduce him to his collar as soon as he comes home to get him accustomed to wearing it. He'll get used to it quickly and won't mind a bit. Make sure that it is snug enough that it won't slip off yet loose enough to be comfortable for the pup. You should be able to slip two fingers between the collar and his neck. Check the collar often, as puppies grow in spurts, and his collar can become too tight almost overnight. Choke collars are for training purposes only and should never be used on a puppy under four or five months old.

LEASHES

A 6-foot nylon lead is an excellent choice for a young puppy. It is lightweight and not as tempting to chew as a leather lead. You can switch to a 6-foot leather lead after your pup has grown and is used to walking politely on a lead. For initial puppy walks and house-training purposes, you should invest in a shorter lead so that you have more control over the puppy. At first, you don't want him wandering too far away from you, and when taking him out for toileting you will want to keep him in the specific area chosen for his potty spot.

Once the puppy is heel trained with a traditional leash, you can consider purchasing a retractable lead. A retractable lead is excellent for walking adult dogs that are already leash-wise. This type of lead allows the dog to roam farther away from you and explore a wider area when out walking, and also retracts when you need to keep him close to you.

HOME SAFETY FOR YOUR PUPPY

The importance of puppy-proofing cannot be overstated. In addition to making your house comfortable for your Black and Tan Coonhound's arrival, you also must make sure that your house is safe for your puppy before you bring him home. There are countless hazards in the owner's personal living environment that a pup can sniff, chew, swallow or destroy. Many are obvious; others are not. Do a thorough advance house check to

Puppies are an inquisitive bunch, always investigating something new. Puppy-proofing your home, indoors and outdoors, is essential to avoiding catastrophes.

remove or rearrange those things that could hurt your puppy, keeping any potentially dangerous items out of areas to which he will have access.

Electrical cords are especially dangerous, since puppies view them as irresistible chew toys. Unplug and remove all exposed cords or fasten them beneath baseboards where the puppy cannot reach them. Veterinarians and firefighters can tell you horror stories about electrical burns and house fires that resulted from puppy-chewed electrical cords. Consider this a most serious precaution for your puppy and the rest of your family.

Scout your home for tiny objects that might be seen at a pup's eye level. Keep medication

There's no telling what kind of mischief your Black and Tan puppy will get into. Keep a sharp eye on your best friend so he doesn't find himself in a precarious situation.

PUPPY SHOTS

Puppies are born with natural antibodies that protect them from most canine diseases. They receive more antibodies from the colostrum in their mother's milk. These immunities wear off, however, and must be replaced through a series of vaccines. Puppy shots are given at 3- to 4-week intervals starting at 6 to 8 weeks of age through 16 to 20 weeks of age. Booster shots are given after one year of age, and every one to three years thereafter.

bottles and cleaning supplies well out of reach, and do the same with waste baskets and other trash containers. It goes without saying that you should not use rodent poison or other toxic chemicals in any puppy area and that you must keep such containers safely locked up. You will be amazed at how many places a curious puppy can discover!

Once your house has cleared inspection, check your yard. A sturdy fence, well embedded into the ground, will give your dog a safe place to play and potty. Although Black and Tan Coonhounds are not known to be climbers or fence jumpers, they are still athletic dogs, so a 5- to 6-foot-high fence should be adequate to contain an agile youngster or adult. Check the fence periodically for necessary repairs. If there is a weak link or space to squeeze through, you can be sure a determined Black and Tan Coonhound will discover it.

The garage and shed can be hazardous places for a pup, as things like fertilizers, chemicals and tools are usually kept there. It's best to keep these areas off limits to the pup. Antifreeze is especially dangerous to dogs, as they find the taste appealing and it takes only a few licks from the driveway to kill a dog, puppy or adult, small breed or large.

VISITING THE VETERINARIAN

A good veterinarian is your Black and Tan Coonhound puppy's best health-insurance policy. If you do not already have a vet, ask friends and experienced dog people in your area for recommendations so that you can select a vet before you bring your Black and Tan Coonhound puppy home. Also arrange for your puppy's first veterinary examination beforehand, since many vets do not have appointments immediately available, and your puppy should visit the vet within a day or so of coming home.

It's important to make sure your puppy's first visit to the vet is a pleasant and positive one. The vet should take great care to befriend the pup and handle him gently to make their first meeting a positive experience. The vet will give the pup a thorough physical examination and set up a schedule for vaccinations and other necessary wellness visits. Be sure to show your vet any health and inoculation records, which you should have received from your breeder. Your vet is a great source of canine health information, so be sure to ask questions and take notes. Creating a health journal for your puppy will make a handy reference for his wellness and any future health problems that may arise.

The Black and Tan Coonhound is surely a gift that keeps on giving.

MEETING THE FAMILY

Your Black and Tan Coonhound's homecoming is an exciting time for all members of the family, and it's only natural that everyone will be eager to meet him, pet him and play with him. However, for the puppy's sake, it's best to make these initial family meetings as uneventful as possible so that the pup is not overwhelmed with too

Don't let children overwhelm your pup upon his arrival to his new home. They will have plenty of time to get to know one another.

the crate; if he associates the crate with food, he will associate the crate with good things. If he is comfortable with the crate, you can offer him his first meal inside it. Leave the door ajar so he can wander in and out as he chooses.

FIRST NIGHT IN HIS NEW HOME

So much has happened in your Black and Tan Coonhound puppy's first day away from the breeder. He's had his first car ride to his new home. He's met his new human family and perhaps the other family pets. He has explored his new house and yard, at least those places where he is to be allowed during his first weeks at home. He may have visited his new veterinarian. He has eaten his first meal or two away from his dam and littermates. Surely that's

much too soon. Remember, he has just left his dam and his littermates and is away from the breeder's home for the first time. Despite his fuzzy wagging tail, he is still apprehensive and wondering where he is and who all these strange humans are. It's best to let him explore on his own and meet the family members as he feels comfortable. Let him investigate all the new smells, sights and sounds at his own pace. Children should be especially careful to not get overly excited, use loud voices or hug the pup too tightly. Be calm, gentle and affectionate, and be ready to comfort him if he appears frightened or uneasy.

Be sure to show your puppy his new crate during this first day home. Toss a treat or two inside

MEET AND MINGLE

Puppies need to meet people and see the world if they are to grow up confident and unafraid. Take your puppy with you on everyday outings and errands. On-lead walks around the neighborhood and to the park offer the pup good exposure to the goings-on of his new human world. Avoid areas frequented by other dogs until your puppy has had his full round of puppy shots; ask your vet when your pup will be properly protected. Arrange for your puppy to meet new people of all ages every week.

enough to tire out an eight-week-old Black and Tan Coonhound pup—or so you hope!

It's bedtime. During the day, the pup investigated his crate, which is his new den and sleeping space, so it is not entirely strange to him. Line the crate with a soft towel or blanket that he can snuggle into and gently place him into the crate for the night. Some breeders send home a piece of bedding from where the pup slept with his littermates, and those familiar scents are a great comfort for the puppy on his first night without his siblings.

He will probably whine or cry. The puppy is objecting to the confinement and the fact that he is alone for the first time. This can be a stressful time for you as well as for the pup. It's important that you remain strong and don't let the puppy out of his crate to comfort him. He will fall asleep eventually. If you release him, the puppy will learn that crying means "out" and will continue that habit. You are laying the groundwork for future habits. Some breeders find that soft music can soothe a crying pup and help him get to sleep.

SOCIALIZING YOUR PUPPY

The first 20 weeks of your Black and Tan Coonhound puppy's life are the most important of his entire lifetime. A properly socialized puppy will grow up to be a confident and stable adult who will be a pleasure to live with and a welcome addition to the neighborhood.

The importance of socialization cannot be overemphasized. Research on canine behavior has

A puppy will get tuckered out just by engaging in normal puppy behavior. Provide your sleepy pal with a comfy place to take a load off.

The puppy's socialization began at the breeder's with his littermates and visitors to the kennel. You must become your puppy's social director once he arrives at your home.

proven that puppies who are not exposed to new sights, sounds, people and animals during their first 20 weeks of life will grow up to be timid and fearful, even aggressive, and unable to flourish outside of their familiar home environment.

Socializing your puppy is not difficult and, in fact, will be a fun time for you both. Lead training goes hand in hand with socialization, so your puppy will be learning how to walk on a lead at the same time that he's meeting the neighborhood. Because the Black and Tan Coonhound is such a terrific breed, everyone will enjoy meeting "the new kid on the block." Take him for short walks, to the park and to other dog-friendly places where he will encounter new people, especially children. Puppies automatically recognize children as "little people" and are drawn to play with them. Just make sure that you supervise these meetings and that the children do not get too

rough or encourage him to play too hard. An overzealous pup can often nip too hard, frightening the child and in turn making the puppy overly excited. A bad experience in puppyhood can impact a dog for life, so a pup that has a negative experience with a child may grow up to be shy or even aggressive around children.

Take your puppy along on your daily errands. Puppies are natural "people magnets," and most people who see your pup will want to pet him. All of these encounters will help to mold him into a confident adult dog. Likewise, you will soon feel like a confident, responsible dog owner, rightly proud of your mannerly Black and Tan Coonhound.

Be especially careful of your puppy's encounters and experiences during the eight to- ten-week-old period, which is also called the "fear period." This is a serious imprinting period, and all contact during this time should be gentle and positive. A frightening or negative event could leave a permanent impression that could affect his future behavior if a similar situation arises.

Also make sure that your puppy has received his first and second rounds of vaccinations before you expose him to other dogs or bring him to places that other dogs may frequent. Avoid dog parks and other strange-dog areas until your vet assures you that your puppy is fully immunized and resistant to the diseases that can be passed between canines. Discuss socialization with your breeder, as some breeders recommend socializing the puppy even before he has received all of his inoculations, depending on how outgoing the breed or puppy may be.

LEADER OF THE PUPPY'S PACK
Like other canines, your puppy needs an authority figure, someone he can look up to and regard as the leader of his "pack." His first pack leader was his dam, who taught him to be polite and not chew too hard on her ears or nip at her muzzle. He learned those same lessons from his littermates. If he played too rough, they cried in pain and stopped the game, which sent an important message to the rowdy puppy.

As puppies play together, they are also struggling to determine who will be the boss. Being pack animals, dogs need someone to be in charge. If a litter of puppies remained together beyond puppyhood, one of the pups would emerge as the strongest one, the one who calls the shots.

Once your puppy leaves the pack, he will look intuitively for a new leader. If he does not recognize you as that leader, he will try to assume that position for himself. Of course, it is hard to

imagine your adorable Black and Tan Coonhound puppy trying to be in charge when he is so small and seemingly helpless. You must remember that these are natural canine instincts. Do not cave in and allow your pup to get the upper "paw"!

Just as socialization is so important during these first 20 weeks, so too is your puppy's early education. He was born without any bad habits. He does not know what is good or bad behavior. If he does things like nipping and digging, it's because he is having fun and doesn't know that humans consider these things as "bad." It's your job to teach him proper puppy manners, and this is the best time to accomplish that—before he has developed bad habits, since it is much more difficult to "unlearn" or correct unacceptable learned

Just as there is a pack order among dogs, there is a pack order in your home. It is up to you to establish yourself as the leader of the household.

If there's something you don't want your pups to have, keep it out of their reach or your little bandits will surely make it their own.

behavior than to teach good behavior from the start.

Make sure that all members of the family understand the importance of being consistent when training their new puppy. If you tell the puppy to stay off the sofa and your daughter allows him to cuddle on the couch to watch her favorite television show, your pup will be confused about what he is and is not allowed to do. Have a family conference before your pup comes home so that everyone understands the basic principles of puppy training and the rules you have set forth for the pup, and agrees to follow them.

The old saying that "an ounce of prevention is worth a pound of cure" is especially true when it comes to puppies. It is much easier to prevent inappropriate behavior than it is to change it. It's also easier and less stressful for the pup, since it will keep discipline to a minimum and

create a more positive learning environment for him. That, in turn, will also be easier on you!

Here are a few commonsense tips to keep your belongings safe and your puppy out of trouble:

- Keep your closet doors closed and your shoes, socks and other apparel off the floor so your puppy can't get at them.
- Keep a secure lid on the trash container or put the trash where your puppy can't dig into it. He can't damage what he can't reach!
- Supervise your puppy at all times to make sure he is not getting into mischief. If he starts to chew the corner of the rug, you can distract him instantly by tossing a toy for him to fetch. You also will be able to whisk him outside when you notice that he is about to piddle on the carpet. If you can't see your puppy, you can't teach him or correct his behavior.

HAPPY PUPPIES COME RUNNING

Never call your puppy (or adult dog) to come to you and then scold him or discipline him when he gets there. He will make a natural association between coming to you and being scolded, and he will think he was a bad dog for coming to you. He will then be reluctant to come whenever he is called. Always praise your puppy every time he comes to you.

SOLVING PUPPY PROBLEMS

CHEWING AND NIPPING

Nipping at fingers and toes is normal puppy behavior. Chewing is also the way that puppies investigate their surroundings. However, you will have to teach your puppy that chewing anything other than his toys is not acceptable. That won't happen overnight and at times puppy teeth will test your patience. However, if you allow nipping and chewing to continue, just think about the damage that a mature Black and Tan Coonhound can do with a full set of adult teeth.

Whenever your puppy nips your hand or fingers, cry out "Ouch!" in a loud voice, which should startle your puppy and stop him from nipping, even if only for a moment. Immediately distract him by offering a small treat or an appropriate toy for him to chew instead (which means having chew toys and puppy treats handy or in your pockets at all times). Praise him when he takes the toy and tell him what a good fellow he is. Praise is just as or even more important in puppy training as discipline and correction.

Puppies also tend to nip at children more often than adults, since they perceive little ones to be more vulnerable and more similar to their littermates. Teach your children appropriate

responses to nipping behavior. If they are unable to handle it themselves, you may have to intervene. Puppy nips can be quite painful and a child's frightened reaction will only encourage a puppy to nip harder, which is a natural canine response. As with all other puppy situations, interaction between your Black and Tan Coonhound puppy and children should be supervised.

Chewing on objects, not just family members' fingers and ankles, is also normal canine behavior that can be especially tedious (for the owner, not the pup) during the teething period when the puppy's adult teeth are coming in. At this stage, chewing

Of course your puppy doesn't mean to do things to displease you, it is just normal puppy behavior! With proper, consistent guidance, your Black and Tan will soon behave like the little gentleman that you desire.

just plain feels good. Furniture legs and cabinet corners are common puppy favorites. Shoes and other personal items also taste pretty good to a pup.

The best solution is, once again, prevention. If you value something, keep it tucked away and out of reach. You can't hide your dining-room table in a closet, but you can try to deflect the chewing by applying a bitter product made just to deter dogs from chewing. Available in a spray or cream, this substance is vile-tasting, although safe for dogs, and most puppies will avoid the forbidden object after one tiny taste. You also can apply the product to your leather leash if the puppy tries to chew on his lead during leash-training sessions.

Keep a ready supply of safe chews handy to offer your Black and Tan Coonhound as a distraction when he starts to chew on something that's a "no-no." Remember, at this tender age, he does not yet know what is permitted or forbidden, so you have to be "on call" every minute he's awake and on the prowl.

You may lose a treasure or two during your puppy's growing-up period, and the furniture could sustain a nasty nick or two. These can be trying times, so be prepared for those inevitable accidents and comfort yourself in knowing that this too shall pass.

JUMPING UP

Although Black and Tan Coonhound pups are not known to be notorious jumpers, they are still puppies after all, and puppies jump up—on you, your guests, your counters and your furniture. Just another normal part of growing up, and one you need to meet head-on before it becomes an ingrained habit.

The key to jump correction is consistency. You cannot correct your Black and Tan Coonhound for jumping up on you today, then allow it to happen tomorrow by greeting him with hugs and kisses. As you have learned by now, consistency is critical to all puppy lessons.

For starters, try turning your back as soon as the puppy jumps. Jumping up is a means of gaining your attention and, if the pup can't see your face, he may get discouraged and learn that he

One way to keep your puppy from chewing up your house is to make sure he always has safe chew toys available to him.

loses eye contact with his beloved master when he jumps up.

Leash corrections also work, and most puppies respond well to a leash tug if they jump. Grasp the leash close to the puppy's collar and give a quick tug downward, using the command "Off." Do not use the word "Down," since "Down" is used to teach the puppy to lie down, which is a separate action that he will learn during his education in the basic commands. As soon as the puppy has backed off, tell him to sit and immediately praise him for doing so. This will take many repetitions and won't be accomplished

quickly, so don't get discouraged or give up; you must be even more persistent than your puppy.

A second method used for jump correction is the spritzer bottle. Fill a spray bottle with water mixed with a bit of lemon juice or vinegar. As soon as your puppy jumps, command him "Off" and spritz him with the water mixture. Of course, that means having the spray bottle handy whenever or wherever jumping usually happens.

Yet a third method to discourage jumping is grasping the puppy's paws and holding them gently but firmly until he struggles to get away. Wait a brief moment or two, then release his paws and give him a command to sit. He should eventually learn that jumping gets him into an uncomfortable predicament.

Children are major victims of puppy jumping, since puppies view little people as ready targets for jumping up as well as nipping.

Puppies jumping up may be cute, but you may not think so when a full-grown Black and Tan comes looking for a hug. Establish proper behavior guidelines early in your dog's life.

It's their way of telling us that they are lonely or in need of attention. Your puppy will miss his littermates and will feel insecure when he is left alone. You may be out of the house or just in another room, but he will still feel alone. During these times, the puppy's crate should be his personal comfort station, a place all his own where he can feel safe and secure. Once he learns that being alone is okay and not something to be feared, he will settle down without crying or objecting. You might want to leave a radio on while he is crated, as the sound of human voices can be soothing and will give the impression that people are around.

Give your puppy a favorite cuddly toy or chew toy to entertain him whenever he is crated.

Just because your Coonhound may often have a dour expression doesn't mean he's always sad. If your pup is whining, take the proper steps to help him overcome this behavior.

If your children (or their friends) are unable to dispense jump corrections, you will have to intervene and handle it for them.

Important to prevention is also knowing what you should not do. Never kick your Black and Tan Coonhound (for any reason, not just for jumping) or knock him in the chest with your knee. That maneuver could actually harm your puppy. Vets can tell you stories about puppies who suffered broken bones after being banged about when they jumped up.

PUPPY WHINING
Puppies often cry and whine, just as infants and little children do.

DIGGING OUT
Some dogs love to dig. Others wouldn't think of it. Digging is considered "self-rewarding behavior" because it's fun! Of all the digging solutions offered by the experts, most are only marginally successful and none are guaranteed to work. The best cure is prevention, which means removing the dog from the offending site when he digs as well as distracting him when you catch him digging so that he turns his attentions elsewhere. That means that you have to supervise your dog's yard time. An unsupervised digger can create havoc with your landscaping or, worse, run away!

You will both be happier: the puppy because he is safe in his den and you because he is quiet, safe and not getting into puppy escapades that can wreak havoc in your house or cause him danger.

To make sure that your puppy will always view his crate as a safe and cozy place, never, ever use the crate as punishment. That's the best way to turn the crate into a negative place that the pup will want to avoid. Sure, you can use the crate for your own peace of mind if your puppy is getting into trouble and needs some "time out." Just don't let him know that! Never scold the pup and immediately place him into the crate. Count to ten, give him a couple of hugs and maybe a treat, then scoot him into his crate.

It's also important not to make a big fuss when he is released from the crate. That will make getting out of the crate more appealing than being in the crate, which is just the opposite of what you are trying to achieve.

COUNTER SURFING

What we like to call "counter surfing" is a normal extension of jumping and usually starts to happen as soon as a puppy realizes that he is big enough to stand on his hind legs and investigate the good stuff on the kitchen counter or the coffee table. Once again, you have to be there to prevent it! As soon as you

BE CONSISTENT

Consistency is a key element, in fact is absolutely necessary, to a puppy's learning environment. A behavior (such as chewing, jumping up or climbing onto the furniture) cannot be forbidden one day and then allowed the next. That will only confuse the pup, and he will not understand what he is supposed to do. Just one or two episodes of allowing an undesirable behavior to "slide" will imprint that behavior on a puppy's brain and make that behavior more difficult to erase or change.

see your Black and Tan Coonhound even start to raise himself up, startle him with a sharp "No!" or "Aaahh, aaahh!" If he succeeds and manages to get one or both paws on the forbidden surface, smack those paws (firmly but gently) and tell him "Off!" As soon as he's back on all four paws, command him to sit and praise at once.

For surf prevention, make sure to keep any tempting treats or edibles out of reach, where your Black and Tan Coonhound can't see or smell them. It's the old rule of prevention yet again.

FOOD GUARDING

Some dogs are picky eaters; others seem to inhale their food without chewing it. Occasionally, the true "chow hound" will become protective of his food, which is

one dangerous step toward other aggressive behavior. Food guarding is obvious: your puppy will growl, snarl or even attempt to bite you if you approach his food bowl or put your hand into his pan while he's eating.

This behavior is not acceptable and very preventable! If your puppy is an especially voracious eater, sit next to him occasionally while he eats and dangle your fingers in his food bowl. Don't feed him in a corner, where he could feel possessive of his eating space. Rather, place his food bowl in an open area of your kitchen where you are in close proximity. Occasionally remove his food in mid-meal, tell him he's a good boy and return his bowl.

If your pup becomes possessive of his food, look for other signs of future aggression, like guarding his favorite toys or refusing to obey obedience commands that he knows. Consult an obedience trainer for help in reinforcing obedience so your Black and Tan Coonhound will fully understand that *you* are the boss.

DOMESTIC SQUABBLES

How well your new Black and Tan Coonhound will get along with an older dog who has squatter's rights depends largely on the individual dogs. Like people, some dogs are more gregarious than others and will enjoy having a furry friend to play with. Others will not be thrilled at the prospect of sharing their dog space with another canine.

It's best to introduce the dogs to each other on neutral ground, away from home, so the resident dog won't feel so possessive. Keep both puppy and adult on loose leads (loose is very important, as a tight lead sends negative signals and can intimidate either dog) and allow them to sniff and do their doggie things. A few raised hackles are normal, with the older dog pawing at the youngster. Let the two work things out between them unless you see signs of real aggression, such as deep growls or curled lips and serious snarls. You may have to keep them separated until the veteran gets used to the

new family member, often after the pup has outgrown the silly puppy stage and is more mature in stature. Take precautions to make sure that the puppy does not become frightened by the older dog's behavior.

Whatever happens, it's important to make your resident dog feels secure. (Jealousy is normal among dogs, too!) Pay extra attention to the older dog: feed him first, hug him first and don't insist he share his toys or space with the new pup until he's ready. If the two are still at odds months later, consult an obedience professional for advice.

Cat introductions are easier, believe it or not. Being agile and independent creatures, cats will scoot to high places, out of the puppy's reach. A cat might even tease the puppy and cuff him from above when the pup comes within paw's reach. However, most will end up buddies if you just let dog-and-cat nature run its course.

Two's company! With a proper introduction, a Black and Tan will be elated to have another coonhound companion to share a home with.

KEEP OUT OF REACH

Most dogs don't browse around your medicine cabinet, but accidents do happen! The drug acetaminophen, the active ingredient in certain popular over-the-counter pain relievers, can be deadly to dogs and cats if ingested in large quantities. Acetaminophen toxicity, caused by the dog's swallowing 15 to 20 tablets, can be manifested in abdominal pains within a day or two of ingestion, as well as liver damage. If you suspect your dog has swiped a bottle of medication, get the dog to the vet immediately so that the vet can induce vomiting and cleanse the dog's stomach.

BLACK AND TAN COONHOUND

Adding a Black and Tan Coonhound to your household means adding a new family member who will need your care each and every day. When your Black and Tan Coonhound pup first comes home, you will start a routine with him so that, as he grows up, your dog will have a daily schedule just as you do. The aspects of your dog's daily care will likewise become regular parts of your day, so you'll both have a new schedule. Dogs learn by consistency and thrive on routine: regular times for meals, exercise, grooming and potty trips are just as important for your dog as they are for you! Your dog's schedule will depend much on your family's daily routine, but remember that you now have a new member of the family who is part of your day every day.

While they will certainly need food, water and a place to sleep, these are just a few of the things that your Coonhounds will need to grow up to live long and happy lives.

FEEDING

Feeding your dog the best diet is based on various factors, including age, activity level, overall condition and size of breed. When you visit the breeder, he will share with you his advice about the proper diet for your dog based on his experience with the breed and the foods with which he has had success. Likewise, your vet will be a helpful source of advice throughout the dog's life and will aid you in planning a diet for optimal health.

FEEDING YOUR PUPPY

Before taking your new puppy home, ask the breeder what type of food he has been feeding the litter and continue the pup on this diet. Should you wish to switch to a different type of food, add small quantities of the new food to his meals. Each day add more of the desired food and decrease the food that you wish to eliminate. The Coonhound needs a balanced diet of dried food mixed with either canned or cooked meat. Coonhounds should never be fed dairy products such as milk, eggs, cottage cheese or yogurt.

The new puppy should be fed three meals a day for the first three months of his life. At approximately three to six months of age, cut back his meals to two per day. Be careful to store your dog's food in proper containers. Opened packages of food not only lose their vitamin value but spores, germs and insects also can contaminate the food when left open.

Children can play a role in caring for your puppy, as long as they are taught precisely how to interact with their young canine pal.

VARIETY IS THE SPICE

Although dog-food manufacturers contend that dogs don't like variety in their diets, studies show quite the opposite to be true. Dogs would much rather vary their meals than eat the same old chow day in and day out. Dry kibble is no more exciting for a dog than the same bowl of bran flakes would be for you. Fortunately, there are dozens of varieties available on the market, and your dog will likely show preference for certain flavors over others. A word of warning: don't overdo it or you'll develop a fussy eater who only prefers chopped beef fillet and asparagus tips every night.

nutritional contents are also listed on food products. The Coonhound needs a varied and well-balanced diet containing proper amounts of proteins, carbohydrates and fats. Vitamins and minerals are also needed for proper growth and development.

Should your Black and Tan Coonhound be food sensitive,

As your Coonhound matures, his dietary needs change as well. Establishing a mealtime routine is vital to properly rearing your pup.

PROPER DIET FOR THE BLACK AND TAN COONHOUND

The Coonhound is a powerful and extremely active dog and will need a nutritional diet rich in protein and grains. There are many fine food products to choose from. You may want to feed your adult Coonhound a mixture of dry food with quality canned food or cooked meat, as canned food provides flavor and adds variety. However, canned foods alone do not provide the full nutritional requirements for this breed.

Take time to read the labels on the packages of food. Ingredients are listed in order of quantity contained within the food, and

DIET DON'TS

- Got milk? Don't give it to your dog! Dogs cannot tolerate large quantities of cows' milk, as they do not have the enzymes to digest lactose.
- You may have heard of dog owners who add raw eggs to their dogs' food for a shiny coat or to make the food more palatable, but consumption of raw eggs too often can cause a deficiency of the vitamin biotin.
- Avoid feeding table scraps, as they will upset the balance of the dog's complete food. Additionally, fatty or highly seasoned foods can cause upset canine stomachs.
- Do not offer raw meat to your dog. Raw meat can contain parasites; it also is high in fat.
- Vitamin A toxicity in dogs can be caused by too much raw liver, especially if the dog already gets enough vitamin A in his balanced diet, which should be the case.
- Bones like chicken, pork chop and other soft bones are not suitable, as they easily splinter.

eliminate corn and other grains from the diet until you can determine if grains are causing the problem. Should allergic conditions continue, ask your veterinarian for advice on proper feeding.

The Black and Tan Coonhound is a dog that often needs additional vitamins and minerals. Vitamins that are more commonly needed in addition to his regular diet are vitamin A and vitamins in the B category, mainly B-2, B-6 and B-12. Vitamins D and E are often needed to supplement proper nutrition. Minerals that are more commonly needed are bone meal calcium, bone meal phosphorus, copper gluconate, iodine, iron and magnesium. Vitamin C, including ascorbic acid, calcium ascorbate, sodium ascorbate and ascorbyl palmitate should not be fed to the Black and Tan Coonhound, as these vitamins can damage the kidneys and the liver.

DIETS FOR THE AGING DOG

A good rule of thumb is that once a dog has reached 75% of his expected lifespan, he has reached "senior citizen" or geriatric status. Your Black and Tan Coonhound will be considered a senior at about 8 years of age; based on his size, he has a projected lifespan of about 10–12 years. (The smallest breeds generally enjoy the longest lives and the largest breeds the shortest.)

What does aging have to do with your dog's diet? No, he won't get a discount at the local diner's early-bird special. Yes, he will require some dietary changes to accommodate the changes that come along with increased age. One change is that the older dog's dietary needs become more similar to that of a puppy. Specifically, dogs can metabolize more protein as youngsters and seniors than in the adult-maintenance stage. Discuss with your vet whether

Your Black and Tan will help you determine how much to feed. Does he always seem hungry, or does he leave some food in the bowl?

you need to switch to a higher-protein or senior-formulated food or whether your current adult-dog food contains sufficient nutrition for the senior.

Watching the dog's weight remains essential, even more so in the senior stage. Older dogs are already more vulnerable to illness, and obesity only contributes to their susceptibility to problems. As the older dog becomes less active and, thus, exercises less, his regular portions may cause him to gain weight. At this point, you may consider decreasing his daily food intake or switching to a reduced-calorie food. As with other changes, you should consult your vet for advice.

Make sure your Coonhound has water indoors and outdoors, especially in warmer climates.

QUENCHING HIS THIRST

Is your dog drinking more than normal and trying to lap up everything in sight? Excessive drinking has many different causes. Obvious causes for a dog's being thirstier than usual are hot weather and vigorous exercise. However, if your dog is drinking more for no apparent reason, you could have cause for concern. Serious conditions like kidney or liver disease, diabetes and various types of hormonal problems can all be indicated by excessive drinking. If you notice your dog's being excessively thirsty, contact your vet at once. Hopefully there will be a simpler explanation, but the earlier a serious problem is detected, the sooner it can be treated, with a better rate of cure.

DON'T FORGET THE WATER!

For a dog, it's always time for a drink! Regardless of what type of food he eats, there's no doubt that he needs plenty of water. Fresh cold water, in a clean bowl, should be freely available to your dog at all times. There are special circumstances, such as during puppy housebreaking, when you will want to monitor your pup's water intake so that you will be able to predict when he will need to relieve himself, but water must be available to him nonetheless. Water is essential for hydration and proper body function just as it is in humans.

You will get to know how much your dog typically drinks in a day. Of course, in the heat or if exercising vigorously, he will be more thirsty and will drink more. However, if he begins to drink noticeably more water for no apparent reason, this could signal any of various problems, and you are advised to consult your vet.

Water is the best drink for dogs. Some owners are tempted to give milk from time to time or to moisten dry food with milk, but dogs do not have the enzymes necessary to digest the lactose in milk, which is much different from the milk that nursing puppies receive. Therefore stick with clean fresh water to quench your dog's thirst, and always have it readily available to him.

EXERCISE

We all know the importance of exercise for humans, so it should come as no surprise that it is essential for our canine friends as well. Now, regardless of your own level of fitness, get ready to assume the role of personal trainer for your dog. It's not as hard as it sounds, and it will have health benefits for you, too.

Just as with anything else you do with your dog, you must set a routine for his exercise. It's the same as your daily morning run before work or never missing the 7 P.M. aerobics class. If you plan it and get into the habit of actually

doing it, it will become just another part of your day. Think of it as making daily exercise appointments with your dog, and stick to your schedule.

As a rule, dogs in normal health should have at least a half-hour of activity each day. Dogs with health or orthopedic problems may have specific limitations, so their exercise plans are best devised with the help of a vet. For healthy dogs, there are many ways to fit 30 minutes of activity into your day. Depending on your schedule, you may plan a 15-minute walk or activity session in the morning and again in the evening, or do it all at once in a half-hour session each day. Walking is the most popular way to exercise a dog (it's good

Your Coonhound will want lots of time to roam around and explore. Unless he is in an adequately fenced yard, however, it is essential that exercise takes place on lead.

The only way for your Coonhound to enjoy time outdoors more is to be accompanied by another canine pal!

remember not to overdo it, as the excess weight is already putting strain on his vital organs and bones. As for highly active dogs, some of them never seem to tire! They will enjoy time spent with their owners doing things together.

Regardless of your dog's condition and activity level, exercise offers benefits to all dogs and owners. Consider the fact that

for you, too!); other suggestions include retrieving games, jogging and disc-catching or other active games with his toys. If you have a safe body of water nearby and a dog that likes to swim, swimming is an excellent form of exercise for dogs, putting no stress on his frame.

On that note, some precautions should be taken with a puppy's exercise. During his first year, when he is growing and developing, your Black and Tan Coonhound should not be subject to stressful activity that stresses his body. Short walks at a comfortable pace and play sessions in the yard are good for a growing pup, and his exercise can be increased as he grows up.

For overweight dogs, dietary changes and activity will help the goal of weight loss. (Sound familiar?) While they should of course be encouraged to be active,

THE BOVINE CANINE

Does your dog's grazing in the back yard have you wondering whether he's actually a farm animal in disguise? Many owners have noticed their dogs eating grass and wonder why! It is thought that dogs might eat grass to settle their stomachs or to relieve upset tummies. Even cats have been known to eat grass for the same reasons! Stomach upset can be caused by various things, including poor digestion and parasites.

Unfortunately, while the grass may make the dog feel better very temporarily, often they vomit shortly after eating it, as grass can be irritating to a dog's stomach lining. Even worse, who knows what he is ingesting along with the grass? He could be swallowing insects, germs or parasites, thus perpetuating the problem. Grass-eating should be discouraged when you catch the dog in the act, and a trip to the vet to determine the underlying cause is in order.

dogs who are kept active are more stimulated both physically and mentally, meaning that they are less likely to become bored and lapse into destructive behavior. Also consider the benefits of one-on-one time with your dog every day, continually strengthening the bond between the two of you. Furthermore, exercising together will improve health and longevity for both of you. You both need exercise, and now you and your dog have a workout partner and motivator.

GROOMING

The Black and Tan Coonhound sheds excessively all year long and requires daily brushing and combing. Daily brushing is effective for removing dead hair and stimulating the dog's natural oils to add shine and a healthy look to the coat. A natural bristle, rubber brush or hound glove can be used for regular routine brushing, and a stripping comb, used occasionally, will remove dead and dry hair from the undercoat. Regular grooming sessions are also a good way to spend time with your dog. Many dogs grow to like the feel of being brushed and will enjoy the daily routine.

The Black and Tan is also a known drooler, and if he is in the house you should have a towel handy that can be used to clean his face.

BATHING

In general, dogs need to be bathed only a few times a year, possibly more often if your dog gets into something messy or if he starts to smell like a dog. Show dogs are usually bathed before every show, which could be as frequent as weekly, although this depends on the owner. Bathing too frequently can have negative effects on the skin and coat, removing natural oils and causing dryness.

If you give your dog his first bath when he is young, he will become accustomed to the process.

Accustom your Black and Tan puppy to the brushing regimen as soon as you bring him home. In no time he will look forward to this special time together.

Wrestling a dog into the tub or chasing a freshly shampooed dog who has escaped from the bath will be no fun! Most dogs don't naturally enjoy their baths, but you at least want yours to cooperate with you.

Before bathing the dog, have the items you'll need close at hand. First, decide where you will bathe the dog. You should have a tub or basin with a non-slip surface. Small dogs can even be bathed in a sink. In warm weather, some like to use a portable pool in the yard, although you'll want to make sure your dog doesn't head for the nearest dirt pile following

The Black and Tan should not need too much primping. A regular once-over will keep him looking shiny and healthy.

WATER SHORTAGE

No matter how well behaved your dog is, bathing is always a project! Nothing can substitute for a good warm bath, but owners do have the option of giving their dogs "dry" baths. Pet shops sell excellent products, in both powder and spray forms, designed for spot-cleaning your dog. These dry shampoos are convenient for touch-up jobs when you don't have the time to bathe your dog in the traditional way.

Muddy feet, messy behinds and smelly coats can be spot-cleaned and deodorized with a "wet-nap"-style cleaner. On those days when your dog insists on rolling in fresh goose droppings and there's no time for a bath, a spot bath can save the day. These pre-moistened wipes are also handy for other grooming needs like wiping faces, ears and eyes and freshening tails and behinds.

his bath! You will also need a hose or shower spray to wet the coat thoroughly, a shampoo formulated for dogs, absorbent towels and perhaps a blow dryer. Human shampoos are too harsh for dogs' coats and will dry them out.

Before wetting the dog, give him a brush-through to remove any dead hair, dirt and mats. Make sure he is at ease in the tub and have the water at a comfortable temperature. Begin bathing by wetting the coat all the way down to the skin. Massage in the shampoo, keeping it away from his face and eyes. Rinse him thoroughly, again avoiding the eyes and ears, as you don't want to get water into the ear canals. A thorough rinsing is important, as shampoo residue is drying and itchy to the dog. After rinsing, wrap him in a towel to absorb the initial moisture. You can finish drying with either a towel or a blow dryer on low heat, held at a safe distance from the dog. You should keep the dog indoors and away from drafts until he is completely dry.

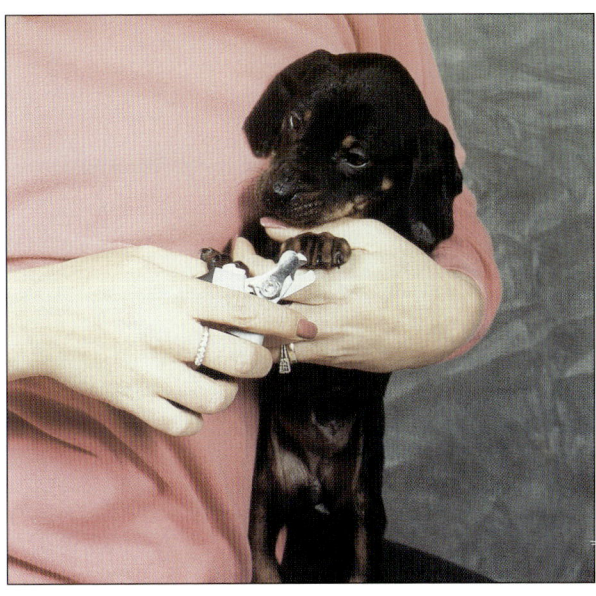

NAIL CLIPPING

Having their nails trimmed is not on many dogs' lists of favorite things to do. With this in mind, you will need to accustom your puppy to the procedure at a young age so that he will sit still (well, as still as he can) for his pedicures. Long nails can cause the dog's feet to spread, which is not good for him; likewise, long nails can hurt if they unintentionally scratch, not good for you.

Some dogs' nails are worn down naturally by regular walking on hard surfaces, so the frequency with which you clip depends on your individual dog. Look at his nails from time to time and clip as needed; a good way to know when it's time for a trim is if you hear your dog clicking as he walks across the floor.

There are several types of nail clippers and even electric nail-grinding tools made for dogs; first we'll discuss using the clipper. To start, have your clipper ready and some doggie treats on hand. You want your pup to view his nail-clipping sessions in a positive light, and what better way to convince him than with food? You may want to enlist the help of an assistant to comfort the pup and offer treats as you concentrate on the clipping itself. The guillotine-type clipper is thought of by many as the easiest type to use; the nail tip is inserted into the opening, and blades on the top and bottom snip it off in one clip.

Start by grasping the pup's paw; a little pressure on the foot pad causes the nail to extend,

A pedicure may not be your Black and Tan's idea of a good time, but if introduced to the nail clipper as a puppy he will learn to tolerate the procedure.

THE MONTHLY GRIND

If your dog doesn't like the feeling of nail clippers or if you're not comfortable using them, you may wish to try an electric nail grinder. This tool has a small sandpaper disc on the end that rotates to grind the nails down. Some feel that using a grinder reduces the risk of cutting into the quick; this can be true if the tool is used properly. Usually you will be able to tell where the quick is before you get to it. A benefit of the grinder is that it creates a smooth finish on the nails so that there are no ragged edges. Because the tool makes noise, your dog should be introduced to it before the actual grinding takes place. Turn it on and let your dog hear the noise; turn it off and let him inspect it with you holding it. Use the grinder gently, holding it firmly and progressing a little at a time until you reach the proper length. Look at the nail as you grind so that you do not go too short. Stop at any indication that you are nearing the quick. It will take a few sessions for both you and the puppy to get used to the grinder.

making it easier to clip. Clip off a little at a time. If you can see the "quick," which is a blood vessel that runs through each nail, you will know how much to trim, as you do not want to cut into the quick. On that note, if you do cut the quick, which will cause bleeding, you can stem the flow of blood with a styptic pencil or other clotting agent. If you mistakenly nip the quick, do not panic or fuss, as this will cause the pup to be afraid. Simply reassure the pup, stop the bleeding and move on to the next nail. Don't be discouraged; you will become a professional canine pedicurist with practice.

You may or may not be able to see the quick, so it's best to just clip off a small bit at a time. If you see a dark dot in the center of the nail, this is the quick and your cue to stop clipping. Tell the puppy he's a "good boy" and offer

a piece of treat with each nail. You can also use nail-clipping time to examine the footpads, making sure that they are not dry and cracked and that nothing has become embedded in them.

The nail grinder, the other choice, is many owners' first choice. Accustoming the puppy to the sound of the grinder and sensation of the buzz presents fewer challenges than the clipper, and there's no chance of cutting through the quick. Use the grinder on a low setting and always talk soothingly to your dog. He won't mind his salon visit, and he'll have nicely polished nails as well.

Ears

In addition, the Coonhound's long pendulous ears are vulnerable to waxy build-up and to collecting foreign matter from the outdoors and can easily become infected.

While keeping your dog's ears clean unfortunately will not cause him to "hear" your commands any better, it will protect him from ear infection and ear-mite infestation. In addition, a dog's ears are vulnerable to waxy build-up and to collecting foreign matter from the outdoors. Look in your dog's ears regularly to ensure that they look pink, clean and otherwise healthy. Even if they look fine, an odor in the ears signals a problem and means it's time to call the vet.

A dog's ears should be cleaned regularly; once a week is suggested, and you can do this

THE EARS KNOW

Examining your puppy's ears helps ensure good internal health. The ears are the eyes to the dog's innards! Begin handling your puppy's ears when he's still young so that he doesn't protest every time you lift a flap or touch his ears. Yeast and bacteria are two of the culprits that you can detect by examining the ear. You will notice a strong, often foul, odor, debris, redness or some kind of discharge. All of these point to health problems that can worsen over time. Additionally, you are on the lookout for wax accumulation, ear mites and other tiny bothersome parasites and their even tinier droppings. You may have to pluck hair with tweezers in order to have a better view into the dog's ears, but this is painless if done carefully.

along with your regular brushing. Using a cotton ball or pad, and never probing into the ear canal, wipe the ear gently. You can use an ear-cleansing liquid or powder available from your vet or pet-supply store; alternatively, you might prefer to use homemade solutions with ingredients like one part white vinegar and one part hydrogen peroxide. Ask your vet about home remedies before you attempt to concoct something on your own.

Keep your dog's ears free of excess hair by plucking it as needed. If done gently, this will be painless for the dog. Look for wax, brown droppings (a sign of ear mites), redness or any other abnormalities. At the first sign of a problem, contact your vet so that he can prescribe an appropriate medication.

A Black and Tan's ears will need to be cleaned often and checked regularly for any foreign matter that could cause potential problems.

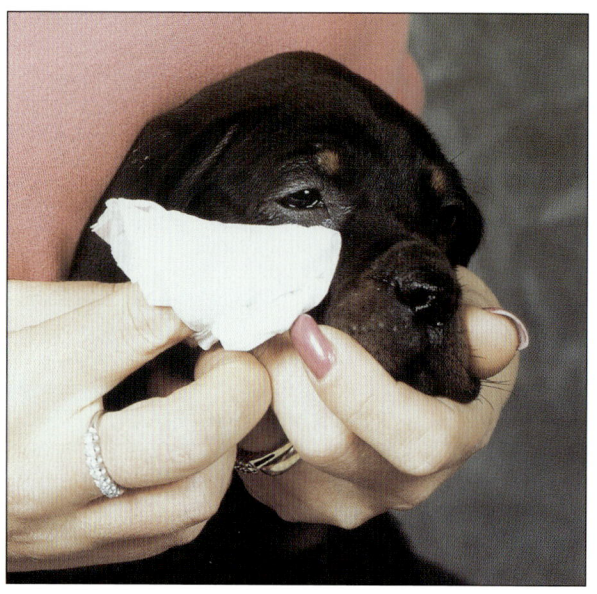

Wiping around the eyes with a cloth and a specially made cleansing solution will remove debris from your Black and Tan's face.

The signs of an eye infection are obvious: mucus, redness, puffiness, scabs or other signs of irritation. If your dog's eyes become infected, the vet will likely prescribe an antibiotic ointment for treatment. If you notice signs of more serious problems, such as opacities in the eye, which usually indicate cataracts, consult the vet at once. Taking time to pay attention to your dog's eyes will alert you in the early stages of any problem so that you can get your dog treatment as soon as possible. You could save your dog's sight!

EYES
The eyes of the Coonhound are loose-lidded and can get infected. Dogs should not be allowed to run in areas where foxtails grow. Foxtails can enter the eye and scratch the cornea or get lodged in the eyes requiring surgical removal.

During grooming sessions, pay extra attention to the condition of your dog's eyes. If the area around the eyes is soiled or if tear staining has occurred, there are various cleaning agents made especially for this purpose. Look at the dog's eyes to make sure no debris has entered; dogs with large eyes and those who spend time outdoors are especially prone to this.

A CLEAN SMILE
Another essential part of grooming is brushing your dog's teeth and checking his overall oral condition. Studies show that around 80% of dogs experience dental problems by 2 years of age, and the percentage is higher in older dogs. Therefore it is highly likely that your dog will have trouble with his teeth and gums unless you are proactive with home dental care.

The most common dental problem in dogs is plaque build-up. If not treated, this causes gum disease, infection and resultant tooth loss. Bacteria from these infections spread throughout the body, affecting the vital organs. Do you need much more convincing to start brushing your dog's teeth? If so, take a good whiff of your dog's breath, and read on.

Fortunately, home dental care is rather easy and convenient for pet owners. Specially formulated canine toothpaste is easy to find.

PRESERVING THOSE PEARLY WHITES

What do you treasure more than the smile of your beloved canine pal? Brushing your dog's teeth is just as important as brushing your own. Neglecting your dog's teeth can lead to tooth loss, periodontal disease and inflamed gums, not to mention bad breath. Can you find the time to brush your dog's teeth every day? If not, you should do so once a week at the very least, though every day is truly the ideal. Your vet should give your dog a thorough dental examination during his annual check-ups.

Pet shops sell terrific tooth-care devices, including specially designed toothbrushes, yummy toothpastes and finger-model brushes. You can use a human toothbrush with soft bristles, but never use human toothpastes, which can damage the dog's enamel. Baking soda is an alternative to doggie toothpastes, but your dog will be more receptive to canine toothpastes with the flavor of liver or hamburger. Make tooth care fun for your dog. Let him think that you're "horsing around" with his mouth. When brushing the dog's teeth, begin with the largest teeth (the canines) and proceed back toward the molars.

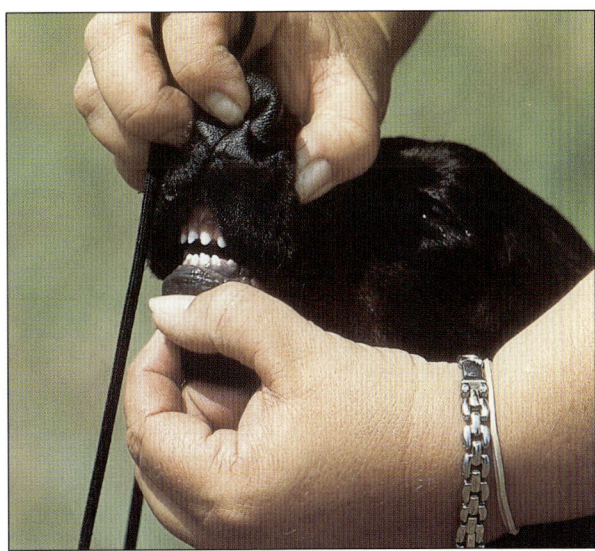

You should use one of these toothpastes, not a product for humans. Some doggie pastes are even available in flavors appealing to dogs. If your dog likes the flavor, he will tolerate the process better, making things much easier for you! Doggie toothbrushes come in different sizes and are designed to fit the contour of a canine mouth. Rubber fingertip brushes fit right on one of your fingers and have rubber nodes to clean the teeth and massage the gums. This may be easier to handle, as it is akin to rubbing your dog's teeth with your finger.

As with other grooming tasks, accustom your Black and Tan Coonhound pup to his dental care early on. Start gently, for a few minutes at a time, so that he gets used to the feel of the brush and

Start handling your Black and Tan's mouth and examining his teeth when he is still young.

to your handling his mouth. Offer praise and petting so that he looks at tooth-care time as a time when he gets extra love and attention. The routine should become second nature; he may not like it, but he should at least tolerate it.

Aside from brushing, offer dental toys to your dog and feed crunchy biscuits, which help to minimize plaque. Rope toys have the added benefit of acting like floss as the dog chews. At your adult dog's yearly check-ups, the vet will likely perform a thorough tooth scraping as well as a complete check for any problems. Proper care of your dog's teeth will ensure that you will enjoy your dog's smile for many years to come. The next time your dog goes to give you a hello kiss, you'll be glad you spent the time caring for his teeth.

THE OTHER END

Dogs sometime have troubles with their anal glands, which are sacs located beside the anal vent. These should empty when a dog has normal bowel movements; if they don't, they can become full or impacted, causing discomfort. Owners often are alarmed to see their dogs scooting across the floor, dragging their behinds behind, this is just a dog's attempt to empty the glands himself.

Some brave owners attempt to evacuate their dogs' anal glands themselves during grooming, but no one will tell you that this is a pleasant task! Thus many owners prefer to make the trip to the vet to have the vet take care of the problem; owners whose dogs visit a groomer can have this done by the groomer if he offers this as part of his services. Regardless, don't neglect the dog's other end Look for scooting, licking or other signs of discomfort "back there" to ascertain whether the anal glands need to be emptied.

IDENTIFICATION AND TRAVEL

ID FOR YOUR DOG

You love your Black and Tan Coonhound and want to keep him safe. Of course you take every precaution to prevent his escaping from the yard or becoming lost or stolen. You have a sturdy high fence and you always keep your dog on lead when out and about in public places. If your dog is not properly identified, however, you are overlooking a major aspect of his safety. We hope to never be in a situation where our dog is missing, but we should practice prevention in the unfortunate case that this happens; identification greatly increases the chances of your dog's being returned to you.

There are several ways to identify your dog. First, the traditional dog tag should be a staple in your dog's wardrobe, attached to his everyday collar. Tags can be made of sturdy plastic and various metals and should include your contact information so that a person who finds the dog can get in touch with you right away to arrange his return. Many people today enjoy the wide range of decorative tags available, so have fun and create a tag to match your dog's personality. Of course, it is important that the tag stays on the collar, so have a secure "O" ring attachment; you also can explore the type of tag that slides right onto the collar.

In addition to the ID tag, which every dog should wear even if identified by another method, two other forms of identification have become popular: microchipping and tattooing. In microchipping, a tiny scannable chip is painlessly inserted under the dog's skin. The number is registered to you so that, if your lost dog turns up at a clinic or shelter, the chip can be scanned to retrieve your contact information.

The advantage of the microchip is that it is a permanent form of ID, but there are some factors to consider. Several different companies make microchips, and not all are compatible with the others' scanning devices. It's best to find a company with a universal microchip that can be read by scanners made by other companies as well. It won't do any good to have the dog chipped if the information cannot be retrieved. Also, not every humane

An identification tag is a necessity for every dog. Be sure it is securely fastened to the collar.

society, shelter and clinic is equipped with a scanner, although more and more facilities are equipping themselves. In fact, many shelters microchip dogs that they adopt out to new homes.

Because the microchip is not visible to the eye, the dog must wear a tag that states that he is microchipped so that whoever picks him up will know to have him scanned. He of course also should have a tag with your contact information in case his chip cannot be read. Humane societies and veterinary clinics offer microchipping service, which is usually very affordable.

Though less popular than microchipping, tattooing is another permanent method of ID

PET OR STRAY?

Besides the obvious benefit of providing your contact information to whoever finds your lost dog, an ID tag makes your dog more approachable and more likely to be recovered. A strange dog wandering the neighborhood without a collar and tags will look like a stray, while the collar and tags indicate that the dog is someone's pet. Even if the ID tags become detached from the collar, the collar alone will make a person more likely to pick up the dog.

dogs' being stolen and sold to research laboratories, but such laboratories will not accept tattooed dogs.

To ensure that the tattoo is effective in aiding your dog's return to you, the tattoo number must be registered with a national organization. That way, when someone finds a tattooed dog a phone call to the registry will quickly match the dog with his owner.

HIT THE ROAD

Car travel with your Black and Tan Coonhound may be limited to necessity only, such as trips to the vet, or you may bring your dog along almost everywhere you go. This will depend much on your individual dog and how he reacts to rides in the car. You can begin desensitizing your dog to car travel as a pup so that it's something that he's used to. Still, some dogs suffer from motion sickness. Your vet may prescribe a medication for this if trips in the car pose a problem for your dog. At the very least, you will need to get him to the vet, so he will need to tolerate these trips with the least amount of hassle possible.

Start taking your pup on short trips, maybe just around the block to start. If he is fine with short trips, lengthen your rides a little at a time. Start to take him on your errands or just for drives around town. By this time it will be easy to tell whether your dog is

for dogs. Most vets perform this service, and there are also clinics that perform dog tattooing. This is also an affordable procedure and one that will not cause much discomfort for the dog. It is best to put the tattoo in a visible area, such as the ear, to deter theft. It is sad to say that there are cases of

water (and food if a long trip) and clean-up materials for potty breaks and in case of motion sickness. Always keep your dog on his leash when you make stops, and never leave him alone in the car. Many a dog has died from the heat inside a closed car; this does

If your car can't accommodate a Coonhound-sized crate, you'll have to explore other options for safe car travel.

a born traveler or would prefer staying at home when you are on the road.

Of course, safety is a concern for dogs in the car. First, he must travel securely, not left loose to roam about the car where he could be injured or distract the driver. A young pup can be held by a passenger initially but should soon graduate to a travel crate, which can be the same crate he uses in the home. Other options include a car harness (like a seat belt for dogs) and partitioning the back of the car with a gate made for this purpose.

Bring along what you will need for the dog. He should wear his collar and ID tags, of course, and you should bring his leash,

DON'T LEAVE HOME WITHOUT IT!

For long trips, there's no doubt that the crate is the safest way to travel with your dog. Luckily, there are some other options for owners who can't accommodate a crate in their cars or whose dogs prove exceptionally difficult to crate-train. In some states, seatbelts are mandatory for humans, and you can consider using the seatbelt on your dog. Purchase a safety harness made for passenger pooches and pull your car's seatbelt through the loop on the harness.

For smaller dogs, consider a car seat made especially for canine passengers. Equipped with their own seatbelts, car seats attach to the seat of the car with the seatbelt.

Larger dogs can be restrained in the rear of the vehicle with a barrier, which you can purchase from a pet store or pet-supply outlet. The barrier is constructed of aluminum, steel or mesh netting. While this device will keep the dog in a designated area, it will not protect him from being jostled about the vehicle on a bumpy ride.

not take much time at all. A dog left alone inside a car can also be a target for thieves.

Up, Up and Away!

Taking a trip by air does not mean that your dog cannot accompany you, it just means that you will have to be well informed and well prepared. The majority of dogs travel as checked cargo; only the smallest of breeds are allowed in the cabin with their owners. Your dog must travel in an airline-approved travel crate appropriate to his size so that he will be safe and comfortable during the flight. If the crate that you use at home does not meet the airline's specifications, you can purchase one from the airline or from your pet-supply store (making sure it is labeled as airline-approved).

It's best to have the crate in advance of your trip to give the dog time to get accustomed to it. You can put a familiar blanket and a favorite toy or two in the crate with the dog to make him feel at home and to keep him occupied. The crate should be lined with absorbent material for the trip, with bowls for food and water attached to the outside of the crate. The crate must be labeled with your contact information, feeding instructions and a statement asserting that the dog was fed within a certain time frame of arrival at the airport (check with your airline). You

will also have to provide proof of current vaccinations.

Again, advance planning is the key to smooth sailing in the skies. Make your reservations well ahead of time and know what restrictions your airline imposes: no travel during certain months, refusal of certain breeds, restrictions on certain destinations. In spite of all of these variables, major carriers have much experience with transporting animals, so have a safe flight.

Dog-Friendly Destinations

When planning vacations, a question that often arises is, "Who will watch the dog?" More and more families, however, are answering that question with, "We will!" With the rise in dog-friendly places to visit, the number of families who bring their dogs along on vacation is on the rise. A search online for dog-friendly vacation spots will turn up many choices, as well as resources for owners of canine travelers. Ask others for suggestions: your vet, your breeder, other dog owners, breed club members, people at the local doggie daycare.

Traveling with your Black and Tan Coonhound means providing for his comfort and safety, and you will have to pack a bag for him just as you do for yourself (although you probably won't have liver treats in your own suitcase!). Bring his everyday items:

food, water, bowls, leash and collar (with ID!), brush and comb, toys, bed, crate, plus any additional accessories that he will need once you get to your vacation spot. If he takes medication, don't forget to bring it with you. If going camping or on another type of outdoor excursion, take precautions to protect your dog from ticks, mosquitoes and other pests. Above all, have a good time with your dog and enjoy each other's company.

BOARDING

Today there are many options for dog owners who need someone to care for their dogs in certain circumstances. While many think of boarding their dogs as something to do when away on vacation, many others use the services of doggie "daycare" facilities, dropping their dogs off to spend the day while they are at work. Many of these facilities offer both long-term and daily care. Many go beyond just boarding and cater to all sorts of needs, with on-site grooming, veterinary care, training classes and even "web-cams" where owners can log onto the Internet and check out what their dogs are up to. Most dogs enjoy the activity and time spent with other dogs.

Before you need to use such a service, check out the ones in your area. Make visits to see the facilities, meet the staff, discuss fees and available services and see whether this is a place where you think your dog will be happy. It is best to do your research in advance so that you're not stuck at the last minute, forced into making a rushed decision without knowing whether the kennel that you've chosen meets your standards. You also can check with your vet's office to see whether they offer boarding for their clients or can recommend a good kennel in the area.

The kennel will need to see proof of your dog's health records and vaccinations so as not to spread illness from dog to dog. Your dog also will need proper identification. Owners usually experience some separation anxiety the first time they have to leave their dog in someone else's care, so it's reassuring to know that the kennel you choose is run by experienced, caring, true dog people.

You should investigate the boarding facilities in your area so that you can choose one with which you are comfortable well before you need it.

BASIC TRAINING PRINCIPLES: PUPPY VS. ADULT

There's a big difference between training an adult dog and training a young puppy. With a young puppy, everything is new! At eight to ten weeks of age, he will be experiencing many things, and he has nothing with which to compare these experiences. Up to this point, he has been with his dam and littermates, not one-on-one with people except in his interactions with his breeder and visitors to the litter.

When you first bring the puppy home, he is eager to please you. This means that he accepts doing things your way. During the next couple of months, he will absorb the basis of everything he needs to know for the rest of his life. This early age is even referred to as the "sponge" stage. After that, for the next 18 months, it's up to you to reinforce good manners by building on the foundation that you've established. Once your puppy is reliable in basic commands and behavior and has reached the appropriate age, you may gradually introduce him to some of the interesting sports,

games and activities available to pet owners and their dogs.

Raising your puppy is a family affair. Each member of the family must know what rules to set forth for the puppy and how to use the same one-word commands to mean exactly the same thing every time. Even if yours is a large family, one person will soon be considered by the pup to be the leader, the alpha person in his pack, the

THE RIGHT START

The best advice for a potential dog owner is to start with the very best puppy that money can buy. Don't shop around for a bargain in the newspaper. You're buying a companion, not a used car or a secondhand appliance. The purchase price of the dog represents a very significant part of the investment, but this is indeed a very small sum compared to the expenses of maintaining the dog in good health. If you purchase a well-bred healthy and sound puppy, you will be starting right. An unhealthy puppy can cost you thousands of dollars in unnecessary veterinary expenses and, possibly, a fortune in heartbreak as well.

"boss" who must be obeyed. Often that highly regarded person turns out to be the one who feeds the puppy. Food ranks very high on the puppy's list of important things! That's why your puppy is rewarded with small treats along with verbal praise when he responds to you correctly. As the puppy learns to do what you want him to do, the food rewards are gradually eliminated and only the praise remains. If you were to keep up with the food treats, you could have two problems on your hands—an obese dog and a beggar.

Training begins the minute your Black and Tan Coonhound puppy steps through the doorway of your home, so don't make the mistake of putting the puppy on the floor and telling him by your actions to "Go for it! Run wild!" Even if this is your first puppy, you must act as if you know what you're doing: be the boss. An uncertain pup may be terrified to move, while a bold one will be ready to take you at your word and start plotting to destroy the house! Before you collected your puppy, you decided where his own special place would be, and that's where to put him when you first arrive home. Give him a house tour after he has investigated his area and had a nap and a bathroom "pit stop."

It's worth mentioning here that, if you've adopted an adult

The rewards of healthy, well-trained Black and Tan Coonhounds are many.

dog that is completely trained to your liking, lucky you! You're off the hook! However, if that dog spent his life up to this point in a kennel, or even in a good home but without any real training, be prepared to tackle the job ahead. A dog three years of age or older with no previous training cannot be blamed for not knowing what he was never taught. While the dog is trying to understand and learn your rules, at the same time he has to unlearn many of his previously self-taught habits and general view of the world.

OUR CANINE KIDS

"Everything I learned about parenting, I learned from my dog." How often adults recognize that their parenting skills are mere extensions of the education they acquired while caring for their dogs. Many owners refer to their dogs as their "kids" and treat their canine companions like real members of the family. Surveys indicate that a majority of dog owners talk to their dogs regularly, celebrate their dogs' birthdays and purchase Christmas gifts for their dogs. Another survey shows that dog owners take their dogs to the veterinarian more frequently than they visit their own physicians.

Working with a professional trainer will speed up your progress with an adopted adult dog. You'll need patience, too.

Some new rules may be close to impossible for the dog to accept. After all, he's been successful so far by doing everything his way! (Patience again.) He may agree with your instruction for a few days and then slip back into his old ways, so you must be just as consistent and understanding in your teaching as you would be with a puppy. (More patience needed yet again!) Your dog has to learn to pay attention to your voice, your family, the daily routine, new smells, new sounds and, in some cases, even a new climate.

One of the most important things to find out about a newly adopted adult dog is his reaction to children (yours and others), strangers and your friends, and how he acts upon meeting other dogs. If he was not socialized with dogs as a puppy, this could be a major problem. This does not mean that he's a "bad" dog, a vicious dog or an aggressive dog; rather, it means that he has no idea how to read another dog's body language. There's no way for him to tell whether the other dog is a friend or foe. Survival instinct takes over, telling him to attack first and ask questions later. This definitely calls for professional help and, even then, may not be a behavior that can be corrected 100% reliably (or even at all). If you have a puppy, this is why it is so very important to introduce your young puppy properly to other puppies and "dog-friendly" adult dogs.

HOUSE-TRAINING YOUR BLACK AND TAN COONHOUND

Dogs are tactility-oriented when it comes to house-training. In other words, they respond to the surface on which they are given approval to eliminate. The choice is yours (the dog's version is in parentheses): The lawn (including the neighbors' lawns)? A bare patch of earth under a tree (where people like to sit and relax in the summertime)? Concrete steps or patio (all sidewalks, garages and basement floors)? The curbside

Puppyhood is the time when you make an impression on your young Coonhound and set the tone for your role as his pack leader.

(watch out for cars)? A small area of crushed stone in a corner of the yard (mine!)? The latter is the best choice if you can manage it, because it will remain strictly for the dog's use and is easy to keep clean.

You can start out with paper-training indoors and switch over to an outdoor surface as the puppy matures and gains control over his need to eliminate. For the naysayers, don't worry—this won't mean that the dog will soil on every piece of newspaper lying around the house. You are training him to go outside, remember? Starting out by paper-training often is the only choice for a city dog.

TIDY BOY

Clean by nature, dogs do not like to soil their dens, which in effect are their crates or sleeping quarters. Unless not feeling well, dogs will not defecate or urinate in their crates. Crate training capitalizes on the dog's natural desire to keep his den clean. Be conscientious about giving the puppy as many opportunities to relieve himself outdoors as possible. Reward the puppy for correct behavior. Praise him and pat him whenever he "goes" in the correct location. Even the tidiest of puppies can have potty accidents, so be patient and dedicate more energy to helping your puppy achieve a clean lifestyle.

WHEN YOUR PUPPY'S "GOT TO GO"
Your puppy's need to relieve himself is seemingly non-stop, but signs of improvement will be seen each week. From 8 to 10 weeks old, the puppy will have to be taken outside every time he wakes up, about 10–15 minutes after every meal and after every period of play—all day long, from first thing in the morning until his bedtime! That's a total of ten or more trips per day to teach the puppy where it's okay to relieve himself. With that schedule in mind, you can see that house-training a young puppy is not a part-time job. It requires someone to be home all day.

Using newspaper in the home can be counterproductive to outdoor training efforts, but you may find it helpful in the beginning stages in case "accidents" occur.

If that seems overwhelming or impossible, do a little planning. For example, plan to pick up your puppy at the start of a vacation period. If you can't get home in the middle of the day, plan to hire a dog-sitter or ask a neighbor to come over to take the pup outside, feed him his lunch and then take him out again about ten or so minutes after he's eaten. Also make arrangements with that or another person to be your "emergency" contact if you have to stay late on the job. Remind yourself—repeatedly—that this hectic schedule improves as the puppy gets older.

HOME WITHIN A HOME
Your Black and Tan Coonhound puppy needs to be confined to one secure, puppy-proof area when no one is able to watch his every move. Generally, the kitchen is the place of choice because the floor is washable. Likewise, it's a busy family area that will accustom the pup to a variety of noises, everything from pots and pans to the telephone, blender and dishwasher. He will also be enchanted by the smell of your cooking (and will never be critical when you burn something). An exercise pen (also called an "ex-pen," a puppy version of a playpen) within the room of choice is an excellent means of confinement for a young pup. He can see out and has a certain amount of space in which to run about, but he is safe from dangerous things like electrical cords, heating units, trash baskets or open kitchen-supply cabinets. Place the pen where the puppy

will not get a blast of heat or air conditioning.

In the pen, you can put a few toys, his bed (which can be his crate if the dimensions of pen and crate are compatible) and a few layers of newspaper in one small corner, just in case. A water bowl can be hung at a convenient height on the side of the ex-pen so it won't become a splashing pool for an innovative puppy. His food dish can go on the floor, next to the water bowl.

Crates are something that pet owners are at last getting used to for their dogs. Wild or domestic canines have always preferred to sleep in den-like safe spots, and that is exactly what the crate provides. How often have you seen adult dogs that choose to

An exercise pen offers the benefits of both housing and control. Once the pup is acclimated, you can use the ex-pen to confine your dog safely indoors and out, whenever the need arises.

DAILY SCHEDULE

How many relief trips does your puppy need per day? A puppy up to the age of 14 weeks will need to go outside about 8 to 12 times per day! You will have to take the pup out any time he starts sniffing around the floor or turning in small circles, as well as after naps, meals, games and lessons or whenever he's released from his crate. Once the puppy is 14 to 22 weeks of age, he will require only 6 to 8 relief trips. At the ages of 22 to 32 weeks, the puppy will require about 5 to 7 trips. Adult dogs typically require 4 relief trips per day, in the morning, afternoon, evening and late at night.

sleep under a table or chair even though they have full run of the house? It's the den connection.

In your "happy" voice, use the word "Crate" every time you put the pup into his den. If he's new to a crate, toss in a small biscuit for him to chase the first few times. At night, after he's been outside, he should sleep in his crate. The crate may be kept in his designated area at night or, if you want to be sure to hear those wake-up yips in the morning, put the crate in a corner of your bedroom. However, don't make any response whatsoever to whining or crying. If he's completely ignored, he'll settle down and get to sleep.

Good bedding for a young puppy is an old folded bath towel or an old blanket, something that is easily washable and disposable if necessary ("accidents" will happen!). Never put newspaper in the puppy's crate. Also those old ideas about adding a clock to replace his mother's heartbeat, or a hot-water bottle to replace her warmth, are just that—old ideas. The clock could drive the puppy nuts, and the hot-water bottle could end up as a very soggy waterbed! An extremely good breeder would have introduced your puppy to the crate by letting two pups sleep together for a couple of nights, followed by several nights alone. How thankful you will be if you found that breeder!

Safe toys in the pup's crate or area will keep him occupied, but monitor their condition closely. Discard any toys that show signs of being chewed to bits. Squeaky parts, bits of stuffing or plastic or any other small pieces can cause intestinal blockage or possibly choking if swallowed.

PROGRESSING WITH POTTY-TRAINING
After you've taken your puppy out and he has relieved himself in the area you've selected, he can have some free time with the family as long as there is someone responsible for watching him. That doesn't mean just someone in the same room who is watching TV or busy on the computer, but one person who is doing nothing other than keeping an eye on the pup, playing with him on the floor and helping him understand his position in the pack.

This first taste of freedom will let you begin to set the house rules. If you don't want the dog on the furniture, now is the time to prevent his first attempts to jump up onto the couch. The word to use in this case is "Off," not "Down." "Down" is the word you will use to teach the down

---

EXTRA! EXTRA!
The headlines read: "Puppy Piddles Here!" Breeders commonly use newspapers to line their whelping pens, so puppies learn to associate newspapers with relieving themselves. Do not use newspapers to line your pup's crate, as this will signal to your puppy that it is OK to urinate in his crate. If you choose to paper-train your puppy, you will layer newspapers on a section of the floor near the door he uses to go outside. You should encourage the puppy to use the papers to relieve himself, and lead him there whenever you see him getting ready to go. Little by little, you will reduce the size of the newspaper-covered area so that the puppy will learn to relieve himself "on the other side of the door."

position, which is something entirely different.

Most corrections at this stage come in the form of simply distracting the puppy. Instead of telling him "No" for "Don't chew the carpet," distract the chomping puppy with a toy and he'll forget about the carpet.

As you are playing with the pup, do not forget to watch him closely and pay attention to his body language. Whenever you see him begin to circle or sniff, take the puppy outside to relieve himself. If you are paper-training, put him back into his confined area on the newspapers. In either case, praise him as he eliminates while he actually is in the act of relieving himself. Three seconds after he has finished is too late! You'll be praising him for running toward you, or picking up a toy or whatever he may be doing at that moment, and that's not what you want to be praising him for. Timing is a vital tool in all dog training. Use it!

Remove soiled newspapers immediately and replace them with clean ones. You may want to take a small piece of soiled paper and place it in the middle of the new clean papers, as the scent will attract him to that spot when it's time to go again. That scent attraction is why it's so important to clean up any messes made in the house by using a product specially made to eliminate the

POTTY COMMAND

Most dogs love to please their masters; there are no bounds to what dogs will do to make their owners happy. The potty command is a good example of this theory. If toileting on command makes the master happy, then more power to him. Puppies will obligingly piddle if it really makes their keepers smile. Some owners can be creative about which word they will use to command their dogs to relieve themselves. Some popular choices are "Potty," "Tinkle," "Piddle," "Let's go," "Hurry up" and "Toilet." Give the command every time your puppy goes into position and the puppy will begin to associate his business with the command.

odor of dog urine and droppings. Regular household cleansers won't do the trick. Pet shops sell the best pet deodorizers. Invest in the largest container you can find.

Scent attraction eventually will lead your pup to his chosen spot outdoors; this is the basis of outdoor training. When you take your puppy outside to relieve himself, use a one-word command such as "Outside" or "Go-potty" (that's one word to the puppy!) as you pick him up and attach his leash. Then put him down in his area. If he is too big for you to carry, snap the leash on quickly and lead him to his spot. Now comes the hard part—hard for

Puppy or adult, it's a good idea to lead your Black and Tan to his "potty spot" on lead until he goes there consistently.

take him back indoors to his confined area and try again in another ten minutes, or immediately if you see him sniffing and circling. By careful observation, you'll soon work out a successful schedule.

Accidents, by the way, are just that—accidents. Clean them up quickly and thoroughly, without comment, after the puppy has been taken outside to finish his business and then put back into his area or crate. If you witness an accident in progress, say "No!" in a stern voice and get the pup outdoors immediately. No punishment is needed. You and your puppy are just learning each other's language, and sometimes it's easy to miss a puppy's message. Chalk it up to experience and watch more closely from now on.

you, that is. Just stand there until he urinates and defecates. Move him a few feet in one direction or another if he's just sitting there looking at you, but remember that this is neither playtime nor time for a walk. This is strictly a business trip! Then, as he circles and squats (remember your timing!), give him a quiet "Good dog" as praise. If you start to jump for joy, ecstatic over his performance, he'll do one of two things: either he will stop mid-stream, as it were, or he'll do it again for you— in the house—and expect you to be just as delighted!

Give him five minutes or so and, if he doesn't go in that time,

KEEPING THE PACK ORDERLY
Discipline is a form of training that brings order to life. For example, military discipline is what allows the soldiers in an army to work as one. Discipline is a form of teaching and, in dogs, is the basis of how the successful pack operates. Each member knows his place in the pack and all respect the leader, or alpha dog. It is essential for your puppy that you establish this type of relationship, with you as the alpha, or leader. It is a form of social coexistence that all canines recognize and accept.

Discipline, therefore, is never to be confused with punishment. When you teach your puppy how you want him to behave, and he behaves properly and you praise him for it, you are disciplining him with a form of positive reinforcement.

For a dog, rewards come in the form of praise, a smile, a cheerful tone of voice, a few friendly pats or a rub of the ears. Rewards are also small food treats. Obviously, that does not mean bits of regular dog food. Instead, treats are very small bits of special things like cheese or pieces of soft dog treats. The idea is to reward the dog with something very small that he can taste and swallow, providing instant positive reinforcement. If he has to take time to chew the treat, he will have forgotten what he did to earn it by the time he is finished!

Your puppy should never be physically punished. The displeasure shown on your face and in your voice is sufficient to signal to the pup that he has done something wrong. He wants to please everyone higher up on the social ladder, especially his leader, so a scowl and harsh voice will take care of the error. Growling out the word "Shame!" when the pup is caught in the act of doing something wrong is better than the repetitive "No." Some dogs hear "No" so often

that they begin to think it's their name! By the way, do not use the dog's name when you're correcting him. His name is reserved to get his attention for something pleasant about to take place.

There are punishments that have nothing to do with you. For example, your dog may think that chasing cats is one reason for his existence. You can try to stop it as much as you like but without success, because it's such fun for the dog. But one good hissing, spitting, swipe of a cat's claws across the dog's nose will put an end to the game forever. Intervene only when your dog's eyeball is seriously at risk. Cat scratches can cause permanent damage to an innocent but annoying puppy.

It is important that the entire family takes part in the training process and uses the same commands in the same manner so not to confuse the dog.

Your Black and Tan will be a willing participant when it comes to training, because it means spending quality time with his favorite person—you!

PUPPY KINDERGARTEN

COLLAR AND LEASH

Before you begin your Black and Tan Coonhound puppy's education, he must be used to his collar and leash. Choose a collar for your puppy that is secure, but not heavy or bulky. He won't enjoy training if he's uncomfortable. A flat buckle collar is fine for everyday wear and for initial puppy training. For older dogs, there are several types of training collars such as the martingale, which is a double loop that tightens slightly around the neck, or the head collar, which is similar to a horse's halter. Do not use a chain choke collar unless you have been specifically shown how to put it on and how to use it. You may not be disposed to use a chain choke collar even if your breeder has told you that it's suitable for your Black and Tan Coonhound.

A lightweight 6-foot woven cotton or nylon training leash is preferred by most trainers because it is easy to fold up in your hand and comfortable to hold because there is a certain amount of give to it. There are lessons where the dog will start off 6 feet away from you at the end of the leash. The leash used to take the puppy outside to relieve himself is shorter because you don't want him to roam away from his area. The shorter leash will also be the one to use when you walk the puppy.

If you've been wise enough to enroll in a puppy kindergarten training class, suggestions will be

BASIC PRINCIPLES OF DOG TRAINING

1. Start training early. A young puppy is ready, willing and able.
2. Timing is your all-important tool. Praise at the exact time that the dog responds correctly. Pay close attention.
3. Patience is almost as important as timing!
4. Repeat! The same word has to mean the same thing every time.
5. In the beginning, praise all correct behavior verbally, along with treats and petting.

READY, SIT, GO!

On your marks, get set: train! Most professional trainers agree that the sit command is the place to start your dog's formal education. Sitting is a natural posture for most dogs, and they respond to the sit exercise willingly and readily. For every lesson, begin with the sit command so that you start out with a successful exercise; likewise, you should practice the sit command at the end of every lesson as well because you always want to end on a high note.

made as to the best collar and leash for your young puppy. I say "wise" because your puppy will be in a class with puppies in his age range (up to five months old) of all breeds and sizes. It's the perfect way for him to learn the right way (and the wrong way) to interact with other dogs as well as their people. You cannot teach your puppy how to interpret another dog's sign language. For a first-time puppy owner, these socialization classes are invaluable. For experienced dog owners, they are a real boon to further training.

ATTENTION

You've been using the dog's name since the minute you collected him from the breeder, so you should be able to get his attention by saying his name—with a big smile and in an excited tone of voice. His response will be the puppy equivalent of "Here I am! What are we going to do?" Your immediate response (if you haven't guessed by now) is "Good dog." Rewarding him at the moment he pays attention to you teaches him the proper way to respond when he hears his name.

EXERCISES FOR A BASIC CANINE EDUCATION

THE SIT EXERCISE

There are several ways to teach the puppy to sit. The first one is to catch him whenever he is about to sit and, as his backside nears the floor, say "Sit, good dog!" That's positive reinforcement and,

Life on the show circuit means frequent travel and competition and thus requires a dog who can follow direction no matter the circumstances.

older) dogs require gentle pressure on their hindquarters with the left hand, in which case the dog should be on your left side. Puppies generally do not appreciate this physical dominance.

After a few times, you should be able to show the dog a treat in the open palm of your hand, raise your hand waist-high as you say "Sit" and have him sit. Once again, you have taught him two things at the same time. Both the verbal command and the motion of the hand are signals for the sit. Your puppy is watching you almost more than he is listening to you, so what you do is just as important as what you say.

It may help to teach the sit by first guiding the puppy into the correct position a few times. Praise him when he assumes a proper sit with your help, and he will soon get the idea and do it on his own.

if your timing is sharp, he will learn that what he's doing at that second is connected to your saying "Sit" and that you think he's clever for doing it!

Another method is to start with the puppy on his leash in front of you. Show him a treat in the palm of your right hand. Bring your hand up under his nose and, almost in slow motion, move your hand up and back so his nose goes up in the air and his head tilts back as he follows the treat in your hand. At that point, he will have to either sit or fall over, so as his back legs buckle under, say "Sit, good dog," and then give him the treat and lots of praise. You may have to begin with your hand lightly running up his chest, actually lifting his chin up until he sits. Some (usually

A happy Coonhound, eager to show he has mastered the sit.

Don't save any of these drills only for training sessions. Use them as much as possible at odd times during a normal day. The dog should always sit before being given his food dish. He should sit to let you go through a doorway first, when the doorbell rings or when you stop to speak to someone on the street.

KEEP IT SIMPLE—AND FUN

Keep your lessons simple, interesting and user-friendly. Fun breaks help you both. Spend two minutes or ten teaching your puppy, but practice only as long as your dog enjoys what he's doing and is focused on pleasing you. If he's bored or distracted, stop the training session after any correct response (always end on a high note!). After a few minutes of playtime, you can go back to "hitting the books."

THE DOWN EXERCISE

Before beginning to teach the down command, you must consider how the dog feels about this exercise. To him, "down" is a submissive position. Being flat on the floor with you standing over him is not his idea of fun. It's up to you to let him know that, while it may not be fun, the reward of your approval is worth his effort.

Start with the puppy on your left side in a sit position. Hold the leash right above his collar in your left hand. Have an extra-special treat, such as a small piece of cooked chicken or hot dog, in your right hand. Place it at the end of the pup's nose and steadily move your hand down and forward along the ground. Hold the leash to prevent a sudden lunge for the food. As the puppy goes into the down position, say "Down" very gently.

The down position will not be your Coonhound's favorite, but he will learn that he should assume the position if it pleases his master.

Have your Black and Tan hold his stay until you give the release word, then reward him with praise and perhaps a treat.

The difficulty with this exercise is twofold: it's both the submissive aspect and the fact that most people say the word "Down" as if they were drill sergeants in charge of recruits! So issue the command sweetly, give him the treat and have the pup maintain the down position for several seconds. If he tries to get up immediately, place your hands on his shoulders and press down gently, giving him a very quiet "Good dog." As you progress with this lesson, increase the "down time" until he will hold it until you say "Okay" (his cue for release). Practice this one in the house at various times throughout the day.

By increasing the length of time during which the dog must maintain the down position, you'll find many uses for it. For example, he can lie at your feet in the vet's office or anywhere that both of you have to wait, when you are on the phone, while the family is eating and so forth. If you progress to training for competitive obedience, he'll already be all set for the exercise called the "long down."

THE STAY EXERCISE

You can teach your Black and Tan Coonhound to stay in the sit, down and stand positions. To teach the sit/stay, have the dog sit on your left side. Hold the leash at waist level in your left hand

DOWN

"Down" is a harsh-sounding word and a submissive posture in dog body language, thus presenting two obstacles in teaching the down command. When the dog is about to flop down on his own, tell him "Good down." Pups that are not good about being handled learn better by having food lowered in front of them. A dog that trusts you can be gently guided into position. When you give the command "Down," be sure to say it sweetly!

and let the dog know that you have a treat in your closed right hand. Step forward on your right foot as you say "Stay." Immediately turn and stand directly in front of the dog, keeping your right hand up high so he'll keep his eye on the treat hand and maintain the sit position for a count of five. Return to your original position and offer the reward.

Increase the length of the sit/stay each time until the dog can hold it for at least 30 seconds without moving. After about a week of success, move out on your right foot and take two steps before turning to face the dog. Give the "Stay" hand signal (left palm back toward the dog's head) as you leave. He gets the treat when you return and he holds the sit/stay. Increase the distance that you walk away from him before turning until you reach the length of your training leash. But don't rush it! Go back to the beginning if he moves before he should. No matter what the lesson, never be upset by having to back up for a few days. The repetition and practice are what will make your dog reliable in these commands. It won't do any good to move on to something more difficult if the command is not mastered at the easier levels. Above all, even if you do get frustrated, never let your puppy know! Always keep a positive, upbeat attitude during training, which will transmit to your dog for positive results.

The down/stay is taught in the same way once the dog is completely reliable and steady with the down command. Again, don't rush it. With the dog in the down position on your left side, step out on your right foot as you say "Stay." Return by walking around in back of the dog and into your original position. While you are training, it's okay to murmur something like "Hold on" to encourage him to stay put. When the dog will stay without moving when you are at a distance of 3 or 4 feet, begin to increase the length of time before you return. Be sure he holds the down on your return until you say "Okay." At that point, he gets

his treat—just so he'll remember for next time that it's not over until it's over.

THE COME EXERCISE

No command is more important to the safety of your Black and Tan Coonhound than "Come." It is what you should say every single time you see the puppy running toward you: "Roscoe, come! Good dog." During playtime, run a few feet away from the puppy and turn and tell him to "Come" as he is already running to you. You can go so far as to teach your puppy two things at once if you squat down and hold out your arms. As the pup gets close to you and you're saying "Good dog," bring your right arm in about waist high. Now he's also learning the hand signal, an excellent device should you be on the phone when you need to get him to come to you! You'll also both be one step ahead when you enter obedience classes.

When the puppy responds to your well-timed "Come," try it with the puppy on the training leash. This time, catch him off-guard, while he's sniffing a leaf or watching a bird: "Roscoe, come!" You may have to pause for a split second after his name to be sure you have his atten-tion. If the puppy shows any sign of confusion, give the leash a mild jerk and take a couple of

Proper leash behavior is important to teach early on, before you have an adult Coonhound taking you for walks.

pleasant and with your approval; then you can rely on his response.

Puppies, like children, have notoriously short attention spans, so don't overdo it with any of the training. Keep each lesson short. Break it up with a quick run around the yard or a ball toss, repeat the lesson and quit as soon as the pup gets it right. That way, you will always end with a "Good dog."

Life isn't perfect and neither are puppies. A time will come, often around ten months of age, when he'll become "selectively deaf" or choose to "forget" his name. He may respond by wagging his tail (and even seeming to smile at you) with a look that says "Make me!" Laugh, throw his favorite toy and skip the lesson you had planned. Pups will be pups!

THE HEEL EXERCISE

The second most important command to teach, after the come, is the heel. When you are walking your growing puppy, you need to be in control. Besides, it looks terrible to be pulled and yanked down the street, and it's not much fun either. Your eight- to ten-week-old puppy will probably follow you everywhere, but that's his natural instinct, not your control over the situation. However, any time he does follow you, you can say "Heel" and be

steps backward. Do not repeat the command. In this case, you should say "Good come" as he reaches you.

That's the number-one rule of training. Each command word is given just once. Anything more is nagging. You'll also notice that all commands are one word only. Even when they are actually two words, you say them as one.

Never call the dog to come to you—with or without his name— if you are angry or intend to correct him for some misbehavior. When correcting the pup, you go to him. Your dog must always connect "Come" with something ahead of the game, as he will learn to associate this command with the action of following you before you even begin teaching him to heel.

There is a very precise, almost military, procedure for teaching your dog to heel. As with all other obedience training, begin with the dog on your left side. He will be in a very nice sit and you will have the training leash across your chest. Hold the loop and folded leash in your right hand. Pick up the slack leash above the dog in your left hand and hold it loosely at your side. Step out on your left foot as you say "Heel." If the puppy does not move, give a gentle tug or pat your left leg to get him started. If he surges ahead of you, stop and pull him back gently until he is at your side. Tell him to sit and begin again.

Walk a few steps and stop while the puppy is correctly

The heel exercise must be mastered by show and pet dogs alike. A show dog must heel at the handler's side while the judge evaluates the dog's gait.

beside you. Tell him to sit and give mild verbal praise. (More enthusiastic praise will encourage him to think the lesson is over.) Repeat the lesson, increasing the number of steps you take only as long as the dog is heeling nicely beside you. When you end the lesson, have him hold the sit, then give him the "Okay" to let him know that this is the end of the lesson. Praise him so that he knows he did a good job.

The cure for excessive pulling (a common problem) is to stop when the dog is no more than 2 or 3 feet ahead of you. Guide him back into position and begin again. With a really determined puller, try switching

LET'S GO!

Many people use "Let's go" instead of "Heel" when teaching their dogs to behave on lead. It sounds more like fun! When beginning to teach the heel, whatever command you use, always step off on your left foot. That's the one next to the dog, who is on your left side, in case you've forgotten. Keep a loose leash. When the dog pulls ahead, stop, bring him back and begin again. Use treats to guide him around turns.

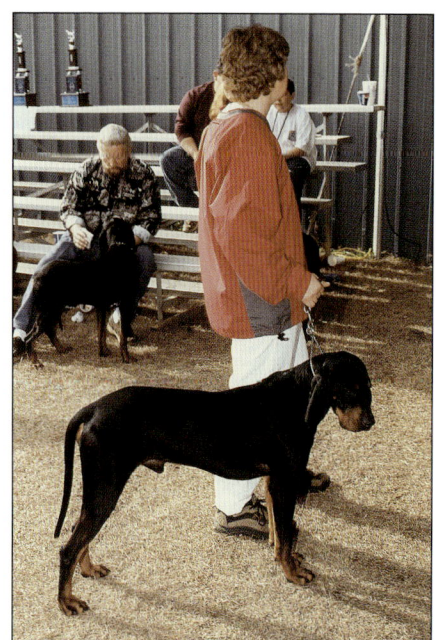

Obedience classes will allow you and your Coonhound to progress to competition if you choose as well as meet some new human and canine friends.

to a head collar. This will automatically turn the pup's head toward you so you can bring him back easily to the heel position. Give quiet, reassuring praise every time the leash goes slack and he's staying with you.

Staying and heeling can take a lot out of a dog, so provide playtime and free-running exercise to shake off the stress when the lessons are over. You don't want him to associate training with all work and no fun.

TAPERING OFF TIDBITS

Your dog has been watching you—and the hand that treats—throughout all of his lessons, and now it's time to break the treat habit. Begin

by giving him treats at the end of each lesson only. Then start to give a treat after the end of only some of the lessons. At the end of every lesson, as well as during the lessons, be consistent with the praise. Your pup now doesn't know whether he'll get a treat or not, but he should keep performing well just in case! Finally, you will stop giving treat rewards entirely. Save them for something brand-new that you want to teach him. Keep up the praise and you'll always have a "good dog."

OBEDIENCE CLASSES

The advantages of an obedience class are that your dog will have to learn amid the distractions of other people and dogs and that your mistakes will be quickly corrected by the trainer. Teaching your dog along with a qualified instructor and other handlers who may have more dog experience than you is another plus of the class environment. The instructor and other handlers can help you to find the most efficient way of teaching your dog a command or exercise. It's often easier to learn by other people's mistakes than your own. You will also learn all of the requirements for competitive obedience trials, in which you can earn titles and go on to advanced jumping and retrieving exercises, which are fun for many dogs. Obedience classes build the foundation

Nordic sled dogs, herding trials for the shepherd breeds and tracking, which is open to all "nosey" dogs (which would include all dogs!). For those who like to volunteer, there is the wonderful feeling of owning a therapy dog and visiting hospices, nursing homes and veterans' homes to bring smiles, comfort and companionship to those who live there.

Around the house, your Black and Tan Coonhound can be taught to do some simple chores. You might teach him to carry a basket of household items or to fetch the morning newspaper. The kids can teach the dog all kinds of tricks, from playing hide-and-seek to balancing a biscuit on his nose. A family dog is what rounds out the family. Everything he does beyond sitting in your lap or gazing lovingly at you represents the bonus of owning a dog.

needed for many other canine activities (in which we humans are allowed to participate, too!).

TRAINING FOR OTHER ACTIVITIES

Once your dog has basic obedience under his collar and is 12 months of age, you can enter the world of agility training. Dogs think agility is pure fun, like being turned loose in an amusement park full of obstacles! In addition to agility, there are hunting activities for sporting and hound dogs, lure-coursing events for sighthounds, go-to-ground events for terriers, racing for the

From hunting to showing, proper training is a necessity that will pave the way to success.

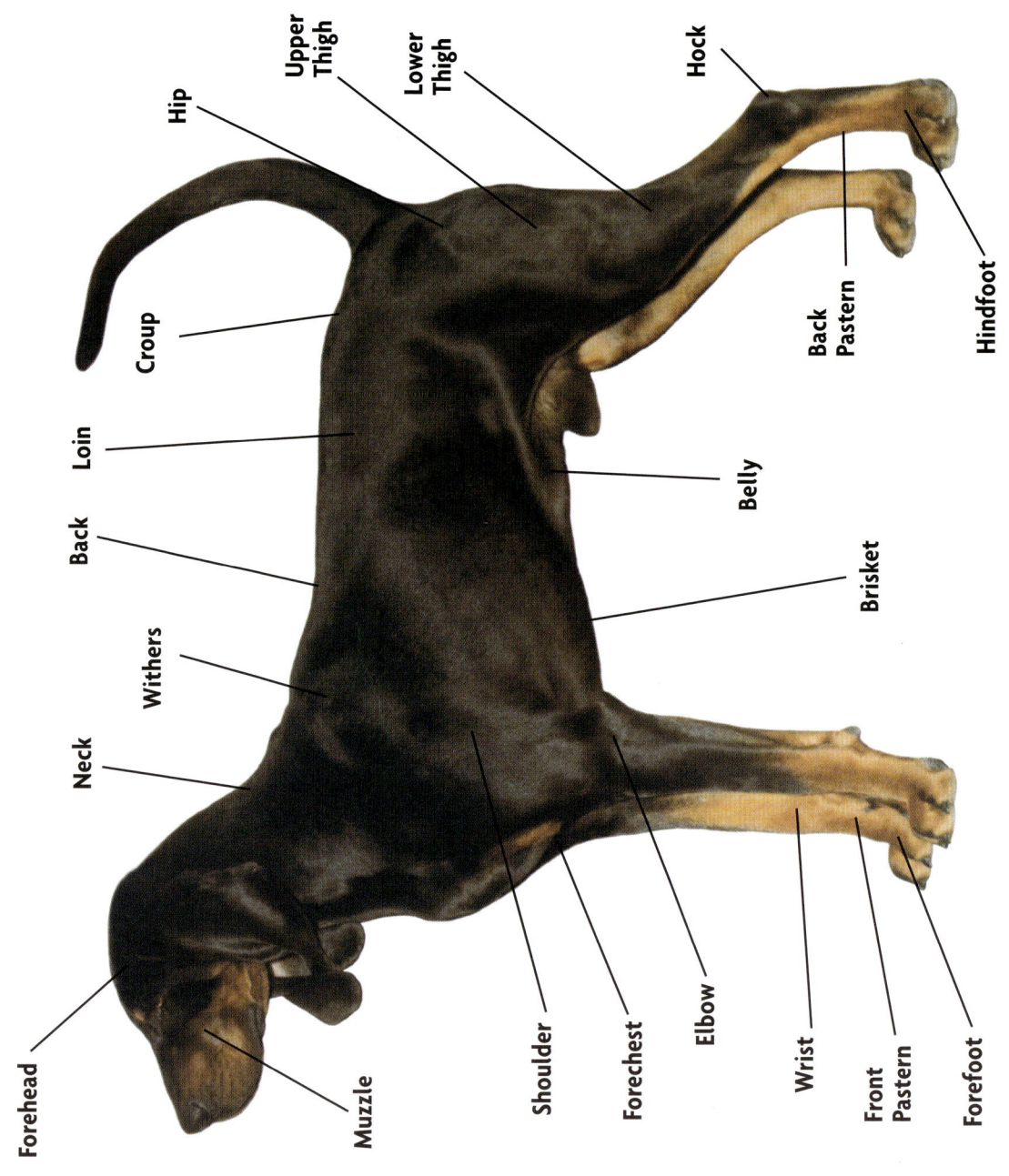

Upper Thigh

Lower Thigh

Hock

Hip

Back Pastern

Hindfoot

Croup

Loin

Belly

Back

Brisket

Withers

Neck

Forehead

Muzzle

Shoulder

Forechest

Elbow

Wrist

Front Pastern

Forefoot

PHYSICAL STRUCTURE OF THE BLACK AND TAN COONHOUND

HEALTHCARE OF YOUR

BLACK AND TAN COONHOUND

BY LOWELL ACKERMAN DVM, DACVD

HEALTHCARE FOR A LIFETIME

When you own a dog, you become his healthcare advocate over his entire lifespan, as well as being the one to shoulder the financial burden of such care. Accordingly, it is worthwhile to focus on prevention rather than treatment, as you and your pet will both be happier.

Of course, the best place to have begun your program of preventive healthcare is with the initial purchase or adoption of your dog. There is no way of guaranteeing that your new furry friend is free of medical problems, but there are some things you can do to improve your odds. You certainly should have done adequate research into the Black and Tan Coonhound and have selected your puppy carefully rather than buying on impulse. Health issues aside, a large number of pet abandonment and relinquishment cases arise from a mismatch between pet needs and owner expectations. This is entirely preventable with appropriate planning and finding a good breeder.

Regarding healthcare issues specifically, it is very difficult to

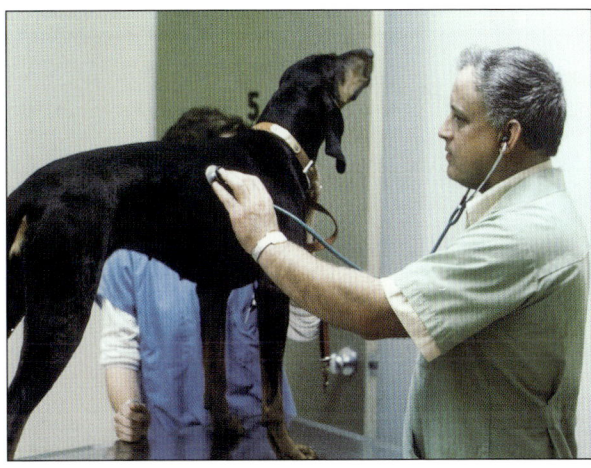

make blanket statements about where to acquire a problem-free pet, but, again, a reputable breeder is your best bet. In an ideal situation you have the opportunity to see both parents, get references from other owners of the breeder's pups and see genetic-testing documentation for several generations of the litter's ancestors. At the very least, you must thoroughly investigate the Black and Tan Coonhound and the problems inherent in that breed, as well as the genetic testing available to screen for those problems. Genetic testing offers some important benefits, but testing is available for

Your veterinarian will provide your Black and Tan with good overall healthcare and alert you to any conditions that require specialized care.

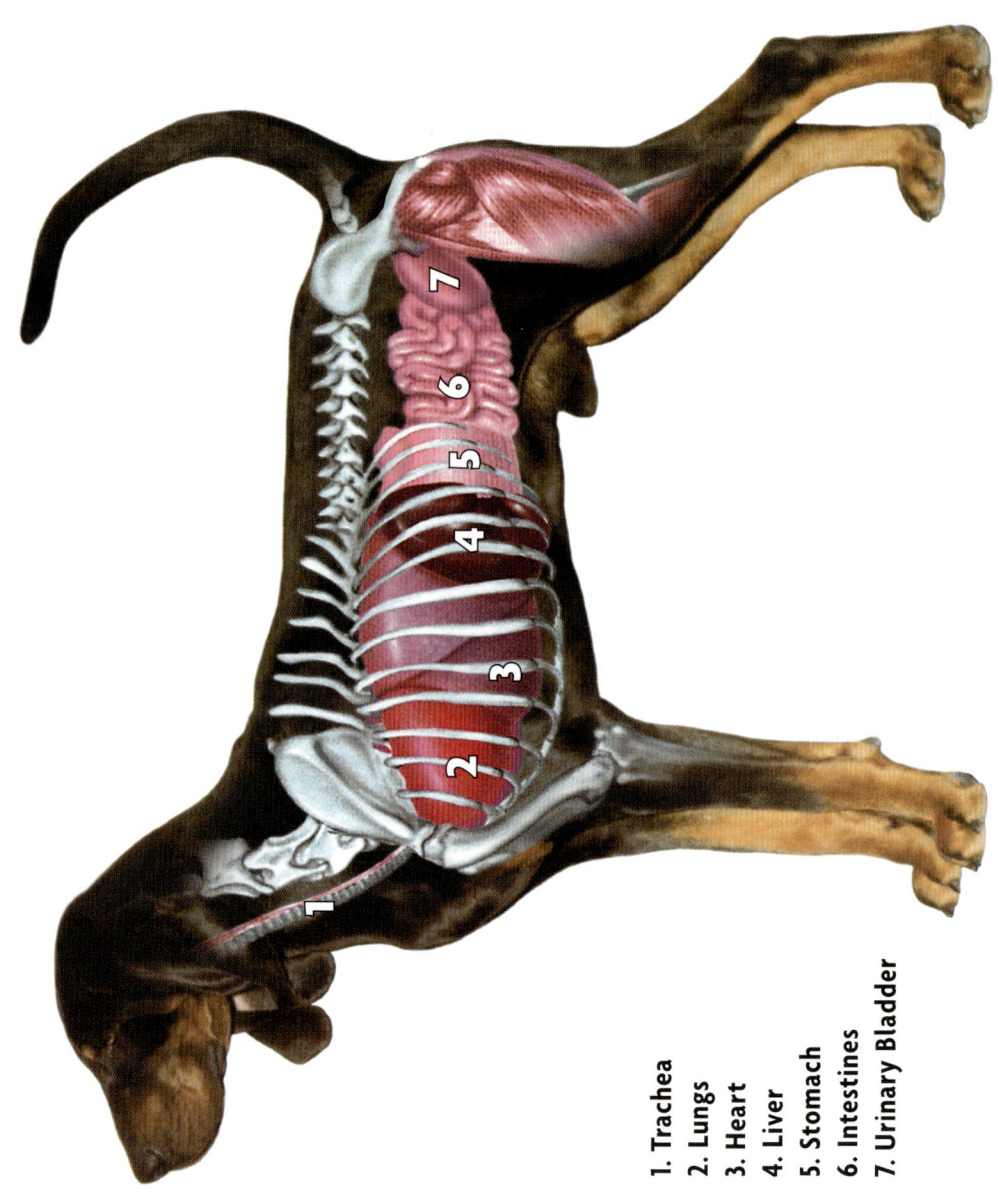

1. Trachea
2. Lungs
3. Heart
4. Liver
5. Stomach
6. Intestines
7. Urinary Bladder

INTERNAL ORGANS OF THE BLACK AND TAN COONHOUND

only a few disorders in a relatively small number of breeds and is not available for some of the most common genetic diseases, such as hip dysplasia, cataracts, epilepsy, cardiomyopathy, etc. This area of research is indeed exciting and increasingly important, and advances will continue to be made each year. In fact, recent research has shown that there is an equivalent dog gene for 75% of known human genes, so research done in either species is likely to benefit the other.

We've also discussed that evaluating the behavioral nature of your Black and Tan Coonhound and that of his immediate family members is an important part of the selection process that cannot be overemphasized. It is sometimes difficult to evaluate temperament in puppies because certain behavioral tendencies, such as some forms of aggression,

may not be immediately evident. More dogs are euthanized each year for behavioral reasons than for all medical conditions combined, so it is critical to take temperament issues seriously. Start with a well-balanced, friendly companion and put the time and effort into proper socialization, and you will both be rewarded with a lifelong valued relationship.

Assuming that you have started off with a pup from healthy, sound stock, you then become responsible for helping your veterinarian keep your pet healthy. Some crucial things happen before you even bring your puppy home. Parasite control typically begins at two weeks of age, and vaccinations typically begin at six to eight weeks of age. A pre-pubertal evaluation is typically scheduled for about six months of age. At this time, a dental evaluation is done (since the adult teeth are now in), heartworm prevention is started and neutering or spaying is most commonly done.

It is critical to commence regular dental care at home if you have not already done so. It may not sound very important, but most dogs have active periodontal disease by four years of age if they don't have their teeth cleaned regularly at home, not just at their veterinary exams. Dental problems lead to more than just bad

HEARTWORM ZONE

Although heartworm cases have been reported in all 48 continental states, the largest threat exists in the Southeast and Mississippi River Valley. The following states have the highest risk factors: Texas, Florida, Louisiana, North Carolina, Georgia, Mississippi, Tennessee, South Carolina, Alabama and Indiana. Discuss the risk factor with your veterinarian to determine your course of prevention for your dog.

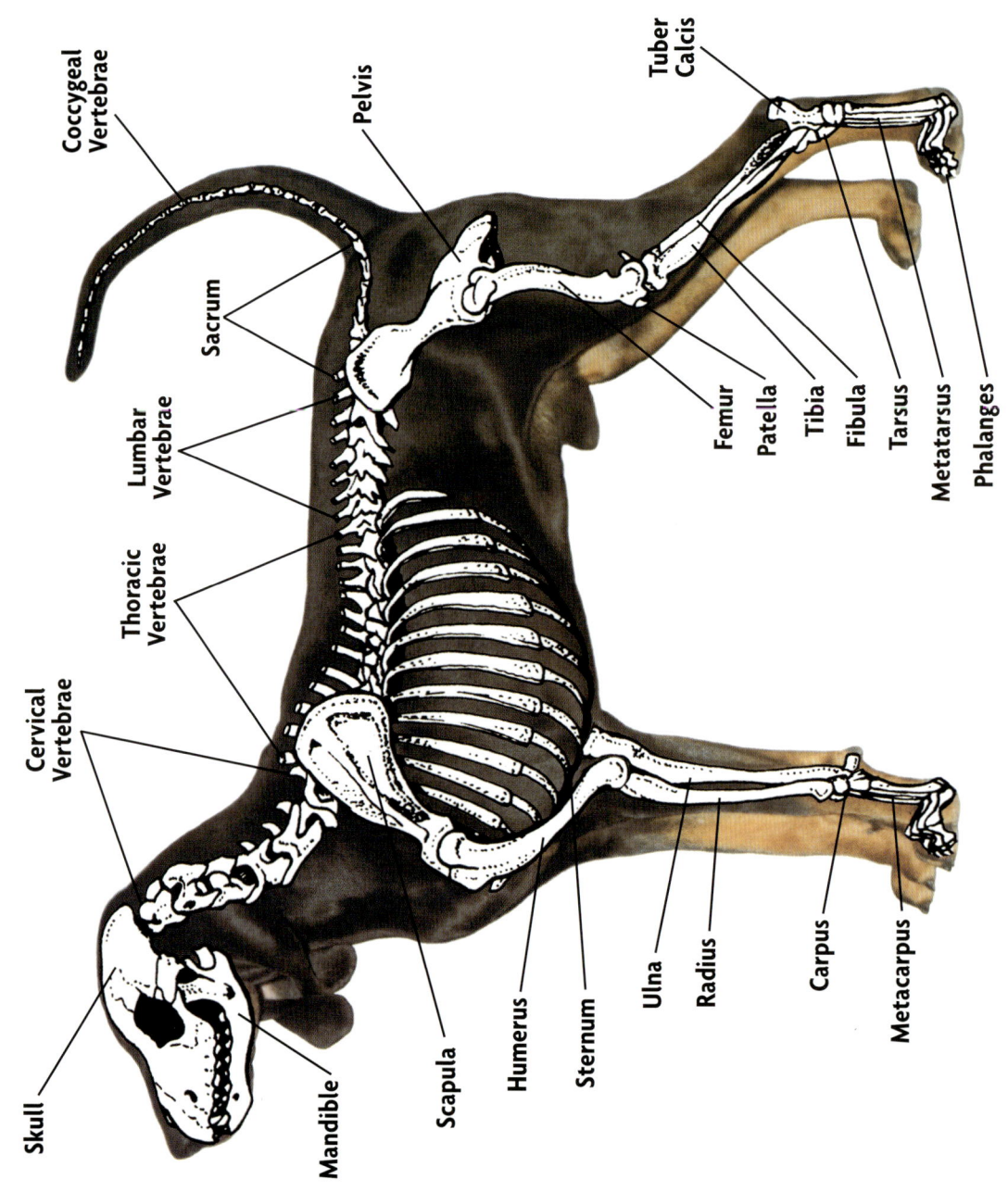

Coccygeal Vertebrae

Pelvis

Tuber Calcis

Sacrum

Femur

Patella

Tibia

Fibula

Tarsus

Metatarsus

Phalanges

Lumbar Vertebrae

Thoracic Vertebrae

Cervical Vertebrae

Skull

Mandible

Scapula

Humerus

Sternum

Ulna

Radius

Carpus

Metacarpus

Skeletal Structure of the Black and Tan Coonhound

"doggy breath." Gum disease can have very serious medical consequences. If you start brushing your dog's teeth and using antiseptic rinses from a young age, your dog will be accustomed to it and will not resist. The results will be healthy dentition, which your pet will need to enjoy a long, healthy life.

Most dogs are considered adults at a year of age, although some larger breeds still have some filling out to do up to about two or so years old. Even individual dogs within each breed have different healthcare requirements, so work with your veterinarian to determine what will be needed and what your role should be. This doctor-client relationship is important, because as vaccination guidelines change, there may not be an annual "vaccine visit" scheduled. You must make sure that you see your veterinarian at least annually, even if no vaccines are due, because this is the best opportunity to coordinate healthcare activities and to make sure that no medical issues creep by unaddressed.

When your Black and Tan Coonhound reaches three-quarters of his anticipated lifespan, he is considered a "senior" and likely requires some special care. In general, if you've been taking great care of your canine companion throughout his formative and adult years, the transition to senior status should be a smooth one. Age is not a disease, and as long as everything is functioning as it should, there is no reason why most of late adulthood should not be rewarding for both you and your pet. This is especially true if you have tended to the details, such as regular veterinary visits, proper

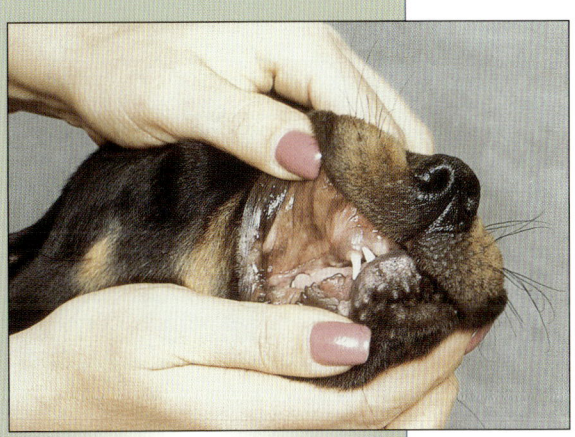

DENTAL WARNING SIGNS

A veterinary dental exam is necessary if you notice one or any combination of the following in your dog:
• Broken, loose or missing teeth
• Loss of appetite (which could be due to mouth pain or illness caused by infection)
• Gum abnormalities, including redness, swelling and bleeding
• Drooling, with or without blood
• Yellowing of the teeth or gumline, indicating tartar
• Bad breath

dental care, excellent nutrition and management of bone and joint issues.

At this stage in your Black and Tan Coonhound's life, your veterinarian may want to schedule visits twice yearly, instead of once, to run some laboratory screenings, electrocardiograms and the like, and to change the diet to something more digestible. Catching problems early is the best way to manage them effectively. Treating the early stages of heart disease is so much easier than trying to intervene when there is more significant damage to the heart muscle. Similarly, managing the beginning of kidney problems is fairly routine if there is no significant kidney damage. Other problems, like cognitive dysfunction (similar to senility and Alzheimer's disease), cancer, diabetes and arthritis, are more common in older dogs, but all can be treated to help the dog live as many happy, comfortable years as possible. Just as in people, medical management is more effective (and less expensive) when you catch things early.

SELECTING A VETERINARIAN

There is probably no more important decision that you will make regarding your pet's healthcare than the selection of his doctor. Your pet's veterinarian will be a pediatrician, family-practice physician and gerontol-ogist, depending on the dog's life stage, and will be the individual who makes recommendations regarding issues such as when specialists need to be consulted, when diagnostic testing and/or therapeutic intervention is needed and when you will need to seek outside emergency and

PROBLEM: AND THAT STARTS WITH "P"

Urinary tract problems more commonly affect female dogs, especially those who have been spayed. The first sign that a urinary tract problem exists usually is a strong odor from the urine or an unusual color. Blood in the urine, known as hematuria, is another sign of an infection, related to cystitis, a bladder infection, bladder cancer or a blood-clotting disorder. Urinary tract problems can also be signaled by the dog's straining while urinating, experiencing pain during urination and genital discharge as well as excessive water intake and urination.

Excessive drinking, in and of itself, does not indicate a urinary tract problem. A dog who is drinking more than normal may have a kidney or liver problem, a hormonal disorder or diabetes mellitus. Behaviorists report a disorder known as psychogenic polydipsia, which manifests itself in excessive drinking and urination. If you notice your dog drinking much more than normal, take him to the vet.

critical-care services. Your vet will act as your advocate and liaison throughout these processes.

Everyone has his own idea about what to look for in a vet, an individual who will play a big role in his dog's (and, of course, his own) life for many years to come. For some, it is the compassionate caregiver with whom they hope to develop a professional relationship to span the lifetime of their dogs and even their future pets. For others, they are seeking a clinician with keen diagnostic and therapeutic insight who can deliver state-of-the-art healthcare. Still others need a veterinary facility that is open evenings and weekends, is in close proximity or provides mobile veterinary services to accommodate their schedules; these people may not much mind that their dogs might see different veterinarians on each visit. Just as we have different reasons for selecting our own healthcare professionals (e.g., covered by insurance plan, expert in field, convenient location, etc.), we should not expect that there is a one-size-fits-all recommendation for selecting a veterinarian and veterinary practice. The best advice is to be honest in your assessment of what you expect from a veterinary practice and to conscientiously research the options in your area. You will

BEWARE THE SPIDER

Should you worry about having a spider spinning her mucilaginous web over your dog? Like other venomous critters, spiders can bite dogs and cause severe reactions. The most deleterious eight-leggers are the black and red widow spiders, brown recluse and common brown spiders, whose bites can cause local pain, cramping, spasms and restlessness. These signals tell owners there is a problem, as the bites themselves can be difficult to locate under your dog's coat. Another vicious arachnid is the bark scorpion, whose bite can cause excessive drooling, tearing, urination and defecation. Often spider and scorpion bites are misdiagnosed because vets don't recognize the signs and owners didn't witness the escape of the avenging arachnid.

quickly appreciate that not all veterinary practices are the same, and you will be happiest with one that truly meets your needs.

There is another point to be considered in the selection of veterinary services. Not that long ago, a single veterinarian would attempt to manage all medical and surgical issues as they arose. That was often problematic, because veterinarians are trained in many species and many diseases, and it was just impossible for general veterinary practitioners to be experts in

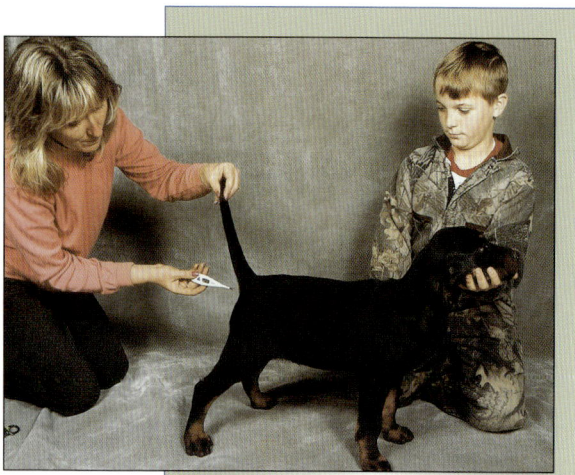

TAKING YOUR DOG'S TEMPERATURE

It is important to know how to take your dog's temperature at times when you think he may be ill. It's not the most enjoyable task, but it can be done without too much difficulty. It's easier with a helper, preferably someone with whom the dog is friendly, so that one of you can hold the dog while the other inserts the thermometer.

Before inserting the thermometer, coat the end with petroleum jelly. Insert the thermometer slowly and gently into the dog's rectum about one inch. Wait for the reading, about two minutes. Be sure to remove the thermometer carefully and clean it thoroughly after each use.

A dog's normal body temperature is between 100.5 and 102.5 degrees F. Immediate veterinary attention is required if the dog's temperature is below 99 or above 104 degrees F.

every species, every breed, every field and every ailment. However, just as in the human healthcare fields, specialization has allowed general practitioners to concentrate on primary healthcare delivery, especially wellness and the prevention of infectious diseases, and to utilize a network of specialists to assist in the management of conditions that require specific expertise and experience. Thus there are now many types of veterinary specialists, including dermatologists, cardiologists, ophthalmologists, surgeons, internists, oncologists, neurologists, behaviorists, criticalists and others to help primary-care veterinarians deal with complicated medical challenges. In most cases, specialists see cases referred by primary-care veterinarians, make diagnoses and set up management plans. From there, the animals' ongoing care is returned to their primary-care veterinarians. This important team approach to your pet's medical-care needs has provided opportunities for advanced care and an unparalleled level of quality to be delivered.

With all of the opportunities for your Black and Tan Coonhound to receive high-quality veterinary medical care, there is another topic that needs to be addressed at the same time—cost. It's been said that you can have excellent healthcare or inexpensive healthcare, but never both; this is as true in veterinary medicine as it is in human medicine. While veterinary costs are a fraction of what the same services cost in the human healthcare arena, it is still difficult to deal with unanticipated medical costs, especially since they can easily creep into hundreds or even thousands of dollars if specialists or emergency services become involved. However, there are ways of managing these risks. The easiest is to buy pet health insurance and realize that its foremost purpose is not to cover routine healthcare visits but rather to serve as an umbrella for those rainy days when your pet needs medical care and you don't want to worry about whether or not you can afford that care.

Pet insurance policies are very cost-effective (and very inexpensive by human health-insurance standards), but make sure that you buy the policy long before you intend to use it (preferably starting in puppy-hood, because coverage will exclude pre-existing conditions) and that you are actually buying an indemnity insurance plan from an insurance company that is regulated by your state or province. Many insurance policy look-alikes are actually discount clubs that are redeemable only at specific locations and for specific services. An indemnity plan covers your pet at almost all veterinary, specialty and emergency practices and is an excellent way to manage your pet's ongoing healthcare needs.

VACCINATIONS AND INFECTIOUS DISEASES

There has never been an easier time to prevent a variety of infectious diseases in your dog, but the advances we've made in veterinary medicine come with a price—choice. Now while it may seem that choice is a good thing (and it is), it has never been more difficult for the pet owner (or the veterinarian) to make an informed decision about the best way to protect pets through vaccination.

Years ago, it was just accepted that puppies got a starter series of vaccinations and then annual "boosters" throughout their lives to keep them protected. As more

Although your veterinarian will recommend which vaccines are necessary for your Coonhound, it's important for you to understand each inoculation and its purpose.

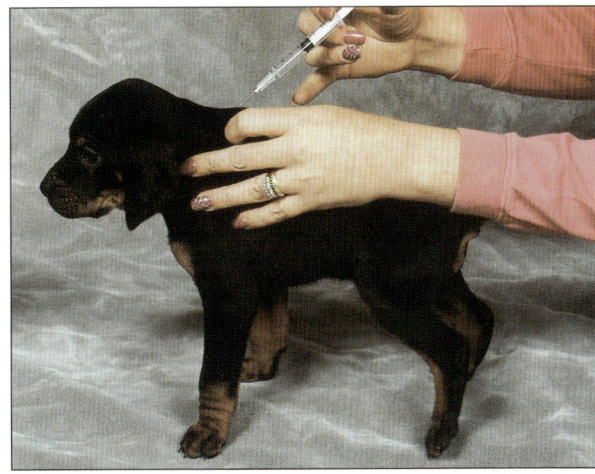

COMMON INFECTIOUS DISEASES

Let's discuss some of the diseases that create the need for vaccination in the first place. Following are the major canine infectious diseases and a simple explanation of each.

Rabies: A devastating viral disease that can be fatal in dogs and people. In fact, vaccination of dogs and cats is an important public-health measure to create a resistant animal buffer population to protect people from contracting the disease. Vaccination schedules are determined on a government level and are not optional for pet owners; rabies vaccination is required by law in all 50 states.

Parvovirus: A severe, potentially life-threatening disease that is easily transmitted between dogs. There are four strains of the virus, but it is believed that there is significant "cross-protection" between strains that may be included in individual vaccines.

Distemper: A potentially severe and life-threatening disease with a relatively high risk of exposure, especially in certain regions. In very high-risk distemper environments, young pups may be vaccinated with human measles vaccine, a related virus that offers cross-protection when administered at four to ten weeks of age.

Hepatitis: Caused by canine adenovirus type 1 (CAV-1), but since vaccination with the causative virus has a higher rate of adverse effects, cross-protection is derived from the use of adenovirus type 2 (CAV-2), a cause of respiratory disease and one of the potential causes of canine cough. Vaccination with CAV-2 provides long-term immunity against hepatitis, but relatively less protection against respiratory infection.

Canine cough: Also called tracheobronchitis, actually a fairly complicated result of viral and bacterial offenders; therefore, even with vaccination, protection is incomplete. Wherever dogs congregate, canine cough will likely be spread among them. Intranasal vaccination with *Bordetella* and parainfluenza is the best safeguard, but the duration of immunity does not appear to be very long, typically a year at most. These are non-core vaccines, but vaccination is sometimes mandated by boarding kennels, obedience classes, dog shows and other places where dogs congregate to try to minimize spread of infection.

Leptospirosis: A potentially fatal disease that is more common in some geographic regions. It is capable of being spread to humans. The disease varies with the individual "serovar," or strain, of *Leptospira* involved. Since there does not appear to be much cross-protection between serovars, protection is only as good as the likelihood that the serovar in the vaccine is the same as the one in the pet's local environment. Problems with *Leptospira* vaccines are that protection does not last very long, side effects are not uncommon and a large percentage of dogs (perhaps 30%) may not respond to vaccination.

Borrelia burgdorferi: The cause of Lyme disease, the risk of which varies with the geographic area in which the pet lives and travels. Lyme disease is spread by deer ticks in the eastern US and western black-legged ticks in the western part of the country, and the risk of exposure is high in some regions. Lameness, fever and inappetence are most commonly seen in affected dogs. The extent of protection from the vaccine has not been conclusively demonstrated.

Coronavirus: This disease has a high risk of exposure, especially in areas where dogs congregate, but it typically causes only mild to moderate digestive upset (diarrhea, vomiting, etc.). Vaccines are available, but the duration of protection is believed to be relatively short and the effectiveness of the vaccine in preventing infection is considered low.

There are many other vaccinations available, including those for *Giardia* and canine adenovirus-1. While there may be some specific indications for their use, and local risk factors to be considered, they are not widely recommended for most dogs.

and more vaccines became available, consumers wanted the convenience of having all of that protection in a single injection. The result was "multivalent" vaccines that crammed a lot of

HIT ME WITH A HOT SPOT

What is a hot spot? Technically known as pyotraumatic dermatitis, a hot spot is an infection on the dog's coat, usually by the rear end, under the tail or on a leg, which the dog inflicts upon himself. The dog licks and bites the itchy spot until it becomes inflamed and infected. The hot spot can range in size from the circumference of a grape to the circumference of an apple. Provided that the hot spot is not related to a deeper bacterial infection, it can be treated topically by clipping the area, cleaning the sore and giving prednisone. For bacterial infections, antibiotics are required. In some cases, an Elizabethan collar is required to keep the dog from further irritating the hot spot. The itching can intensify and the pain becomes worse. Medicated shampoos and cool compresses, drying agents and topical steroids may be prescribed by your vet as well.

Hot spots can be caused by fleas, an allergy, an ear infection, anal sac problems, mange or a foreign irritant. Likewise, they can be linked to psychoses. The underlying problem must be addressed in addition to the hot spot itself.

protection into a single syringe. The manufacturers' recommendations were to give the vaccines annually, and this was a simple enough protocol to follow. However, as veterinary medicine has become more sophisticated and we have started looking more at healthcare quandaries rather than convenience, it became necessary to reevaluate the situation and deal with some tough questions. It is important to realize that whether or not to use a particular vaccine depends on the risk of contracting the disease against which it protects, the severity of the disease if it is contracted, the duration of immunity provided by the vaccine, the safety of the product and the needs of the individual animal. In a very general sense, rabies, distemper, hepatitis and parvovirus are considered core vaccine needs, while parainfluenza, *Bordetella bronchiseptica*, leptospirosis, coronavirus and borreliosis (Lyme disease) are considered non-core needs and best reserved for animals that demonstrate reasonable risk of contracting the diseases.

NEUTERING/SPAYING

Sterilization procedures (neutering for males/spaying for females) are meant to accomplish several purposes. While the underlying premise is to address the risk of pet overpopulation, there are also some medical and behavioral benefits to the surgeries as well. For females, spaying prior to the first estrus (heat cycle) leads to a marked reduction in the risk of mammary cancer and other serious female health problems. There also will be no manifestations of "heat" to attract male dogs and no bleeding in the house. For males, there is prevention of testicular cancer and a reduction in the risk of prostate problems. In both sexes there may be some limited reduction in aggressive behaviors toward other dogs, and some diminishing of urine marking, roaming and mounting.

While neutering and spaying do indeed prevent animals from contributing to pet overpopulation, even no-cost and low-cost neutering options have not eliminated the problem. Perhaps one of the main reasons for this is that individuals that intentionally breed their dogs and those that allow their animals to run at large are the main causes of unwanted offspring. Also, animals in shelters are often there because they were abandoned or relinquished, not because they came from unplanned matings. Neutering/spaying is important, but it should be considered in the context of the real causes of animals ending up in shelters and eventually being euthanized.

One of the important considerations regarding neutering is that it is a surgical procedure. This sometimes gets lost in discussions of low-cost procedures and commoditization of the process. In females, spaying is specifically referred to as an ovariohysterectomy. In this procedure, a midline incision is made in the abdomen and the entire uterus and both ovaries are surgically removed. While

PSEUDOPREGNANCY

Your female dog can experience a pseudopregnancy if she is not bred during her estrus cycle. This pseudocyesis usually occurs about eight weeks after her period and is accompanied by swollen mammary glands and an enlarged abdomen. Your bitch may "adopt" one of her toys as her litter and demonstrate nesting behavior (digging a burrow in your couch or her bed). She may also exhibit aggressive behavior toward humans who attempt to threaten her "litter."

Pseudocyesis may trace back to wolf behavior in the wild. Commonly the aunts or granddam of a litter will assist another bitch in the pack with her litter. All of the bitches will feed the pups and protect them.

Since there are health risks involved with pseudopregnancy, owners are advised to spay their bitches to prevent a recurrence. Bitches can suffer from uterine infections, which can threaten their lives.

this is a major invasive surgical procedure, it usually has few complications, because it is typically performed on healthy young animals. However, it is major surgery, as any woman who has undergone the procedure will attest.

In males, neutering has traditionally referred to castration, which involves the surgical removal of both testicles. While still a significant piece of surgery, there is not the abdominal exposure that is required in the female surgery. In addition, there is now a chemical sterilization option, in which a solution is injected into each testicle, leading to atrophy of the sperm-producing cells. This can typically be done under sedation rather than full anesthesia. This is a relatively new approach, and there are no long-term clinical studies yet available.

Neutering/spaying is typically done around six months of age at most veterinary hospitals, although techniques have been pioneered to perform the procedures in animals as young as eight weeks of age. In general, the surgeries on the very young animals are done for the specific reason of sterilizing them before they go to their new homes. This is done in some shelter hospitals for assurance that the animals will definitely not produce any pups. Otherwise, these organiza-

SPAY'S THE WAY

Although spaying a female dog qualifies as major surgery—an ovariohysterectomy, in fact—this procedure is regarded as routine when performed by a qualified veterinarian on a healthy dog. The advantages to spaying a bitch are many and great. Spayed dogs do not develop uterine cancer or any life-threatening diseases of the genitals. Likewise, spayed dogs are at a significantly reduced risk of breast cancer. Bitches (and owners) are relieved of the demands of heat cycles. A spayed bitch will not leave bloody stains on your furniture during estrus, and you will not have to contend with single-minded macho males trying to climb your fence in order to seduce her. The spayed bitch's coat will not show the ill effects of her estrogen level's climbing such as a dull, lackluster outer coat or patches of hairlessness.

tions need to rely on owners to comply with their wishes to have the animals "altered" at a later date, something that does not always happen.

There are some exciting immunocontraceptive "vaccines" currently under development, and there may be a time when contraception in pets will not require surgical procedures. We anxiously await these developments.

S. E. M. by Dr. Dennis Kunkel, University of Hawaii.

A scanning electron micrograph of a dog flea, *Ctenocephalides canis,* on dog hair.

EXTERNAL PARASITES

FLEAS

Fleas have been around for millions of years and, while we have better tools now for controlling them than at any time in the past, there still is little chance that they will end up on an endangered species list. Actually, they are very well adapted to living on our pets, and they continue to adapt as we make advances.

The female flea can consume 15 times her weight in blood during active reproduction and can lay as many as 40 eggs a day. These eggs are very resistant to the effects of insecticides. They hatch into larvae, which then mature and spin cocoons. The immature fleas reside in this pupal stage until the time is right for feeding. This pupal stage is also very resistant to the effects of insecticides, and pupae can last in the environment without feeding for many months. Newly emergent fleas are attracted to animals by the warmth of the animals' bodies, movement and exhaled carbon dioxide. However, when they first emerge from their cocoons, they orient towards light; thus when an animal passes between a flea and the light source, casting a shadow, the flea pounces and starts to feed. If the animal turns out to be a dog or cat, the reproductive cycle continues. If the flea lands on another type of animal, including a person, the flea will bite but will then look for a more appropriate host. An emerging adult flea can survive without feeding for up to 12 months but, once it tastes blood, it can survive off its host for only 3 to 4 days.

It was once thought that fleas spend most of their lives in the environment, but we now know that fleas won't willingly jump off a dog unless leaping to another dog or when physically removed by brushing, bathing or other manipulation. Flea eggs, on the other hand, are shiny and smooth, and they roll off the animal and into the environment. The eggs, larvae and pupae then exist in the environment, but once the adult finds a susceptible animal, it's home sweet home until the flea is forced to seek refuge elsewhere.

Since adult fleas live on the animal and immature forms survive in the environment, a successful treatment plan must address all stages of the flea life cycle. There are now several safe and effective flea-control products that can be applied on a monthly

> ## FLEA PREVENTION FOR YOUR DOG
> - Discuss with your veterinarian the safest product to protect your dog, likely in the form of a monthly tablet or a liquid preparation placed on the back of the dog's neck.
> - For dogs suffering from flea-bite dermatitis, a shampoo or topical insecticide treatment is required.
> - Your lawn and property should be sprayed with an insecticide designed to kill fleas and ticks that lurk outdoors.
> - Using a flea comb, check the dog's coat regularly for any signs of parasites.
> - Practice good housekeeping. Vacuum floors, carpets and furniture regularly, especially in the areas that the dog frequents, and wash the dog's bedding weekly.
> - Follow up house-cleaning with carpet shampoos and sprays to rid the house of fleas at all stages of development. Insect growth regulators are the safest option.

basis. These include fipronil, imidacloprid, selamectin and permethrin (found in several formulations). Most of these products have significant flea-killing rates within 24 hours. However, none of them will control the immature forms in the environment. To accomplish this, there are a variety of insect growth regulators that can be sprayed into

THE FLEA'S LIFE CYCLE

What came first, the flea or the egg? This age-old mystery is more difficult to comprehend than the actual cycle of the flea. Fleas usually live only about four months. A female can lay 2,000 eggs in her lifetime.

PHOTO BY CAROLINA BIOLOGICAL SUPPLY CO.

Egg

After ten days of rolling around your carpet or under your furniture, the eggs hatch into larvae, which feed on various and sundry debris. In days or months, depending on the climate, the larvae spin cocoons and develop into the pupal or nymph stage, which quickly develop into fleas.

Larva

PHOTO BY CAROLINA BIOLOGICAL SUPPLY CO.

Pupa

These immature fleas must locate a host within 10 to 14 days or they will die. Only about 1% of the flea population exist as adult fleas, while the other 99% exist as eggs, larvae or pupae.

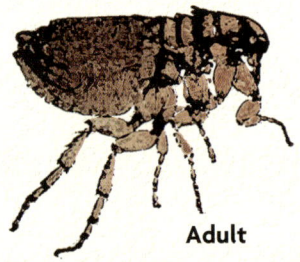

Adult

the environment (e.g., pyriproxyfen, methoprene, fenoxycarb) as well as insect development inhibitors such as lufenuron that can be administered. These compounds have no effect on adult fleas, but they stop immature forms from developing into adults. In years gone by, we relied heavily on toxic insecticides (such as organophosphates, organochlorines and carbamates) to manage the flea problem, but today's options are not only much safer to use on our pets but also safer for the environment.

TICKS

Ticks are members of the spider class (arachnids) and are blood-sucking parasites capable of transmitting a variety of diseases, including Lyme disease, ehrlichiosis, babesiosis and Rocky Mountain spotted fever. It's easy to see ticks on your own skin, but it is more of a challenge when your furry companion is affected. Whenever you happen to be planning a stroll in a tick-infested area (especially forests, grassy or wooded areas or parks) be prepared to do a thorough inspection of your dog afterward to search for ticks. Ticks can be tricky, so make sure you spend time looking in the ears, between the toes and everywhere else where a tick might hide. Ticks need to be attached for 24–72 hours before they transmit most of the diseases that they carry, so you do have a window of opportunity for some preventive intervention.

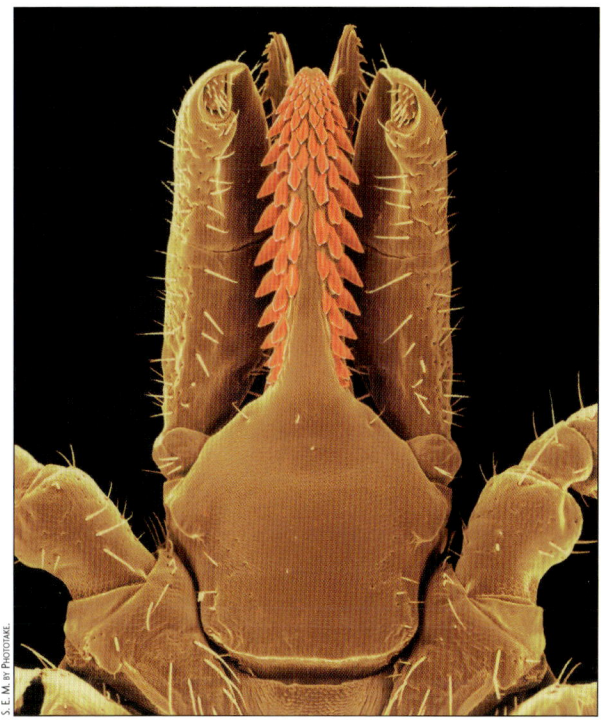

S. E. M. BY PHOTOTAKE.

A scanning electron micrograph of the head of a female deer tick, *Ixodes dammini*, a parasitic tick that carries Lyme disease.

A TICKING BOMB

There is nothing good about a tick's harpooning his nose into your dog's skin. Among the diseases caused by ticks are Rocky Mountain spotted fever, canine ehrlichiosis, canine babesiosis, canine hepatozoonosis and Lyme disease. If a dog is allergic to the saliva of a female wood tick, he can develop tick paralysis.

Female ticks live to eat and breed. They can lay between 4,000 and 5,000 eggs and they die soon after. Males, on the other hand, live only to mate with the females and continue the process as long as they are able. Most ticks live on multiple hosts before parasitizing dogs. The immature forms typically reside on grass and shrubs, waiting for susceptible animals to walk by. The larvae and nymph stages typically feed on wildlife.

If only a few ticks are present on a dog, they can be plucked out, but it is important to remove the entire head and mouthparts,

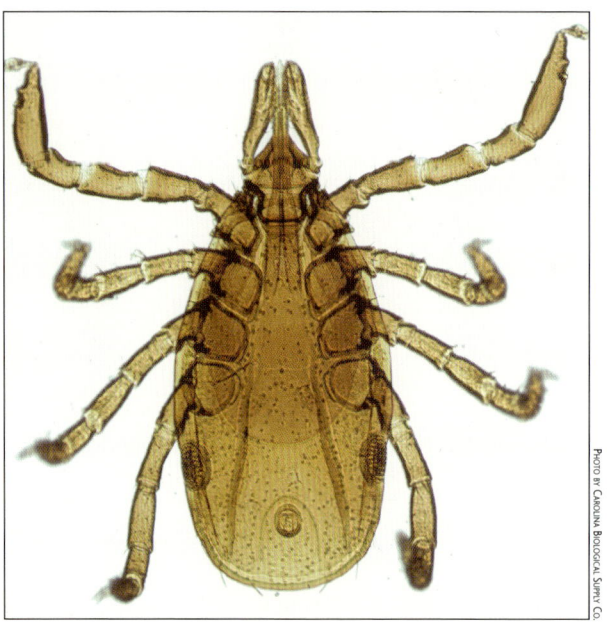

PHOTO BY CAROLINA BIOLOGICAL SUPPLY CO.

Deer tick,
Ixodes dammini.

which may be deeply embedded in the skin. This is best accomplished with forceps designed especially for this purpose; fingers can be used but should be protected with rubber gloves, plastic wrap or at least a paper towel. The tick should be grasped as closely as possible to the animal's skin and should be pulled upward with steady, even pressure. Do not squeeze, crush or puncture the body of the tick or you risk exposure to any disease carried by that tick. Once the ticks have been removed, the sites of attachment should be disinfected. Your hands should then be washed with soap and water to further minimize risk of contagion. The tick should be disposed

of in a container of alcohol or household bleach.

Some of the newer flea products, specifically those with fipronil, selamectin and permethrin, have effect against some, but not all, species of tick. Flea collars containing appropriate pesticides (e.g., propoxur, chlorfenvinphos) can aid in tick control. In most areas, such collars should be placed on animals in March, at the beginning of the tick season, and changed regularly. Leaving the collar on when the pesticide level is waning invites the development of resistance. Amitraz collars are also good for tick control, and the active ingredient does not interfere with other flea-control products. The ingredient helps prevent the attachment of ticks to the skin and will cause those ticks already on the skin to detach themselves.

TICK CONTROL

Removal of underbrush and leaf litter and the thinning of trees in areas where tick control is desired are recommended. These actions remove the cover and food sources for small animals that serve as hosts for ticks. With continued mowing of grasses in these areas, the probability of ticks' surviving is further reduced. A variety of insecticide ingredients (e.g., resmethrin, carbaryl, permethrin, chlorpyrifos, dioxathion and allethrin) are registered for tick control around the home.

MITES

Mites are tiny arachnid parasites that parasitize the skin of dogs. Skin diseases caused by mites are referred to as "mange," and there are many different forms seen in dogs. These forms are very different from one another, each one warranting an individual description.

Sarcoptic mange, or scabies, is one of the itchiest conditions that affects dogs. The microscopic *Sarcoptes* mites burrow into the superficial layers of the skin and can drive dogs crazy with itchiness. They are also communicable to people, although they can't complete their reproductive cycle on people. In addition to being tiny, the mites also are often difficult to find when trying to make a diagnosis. Skin scrapings from multiple areas are examined microscopically but, even then, sometimes the mites cannot be found.

Fortunately, scabies is relatively easy to treat, and there are a variety of products that will successfully kill the mites. Since the mites can't live in the environment for very long without feeding, a complete cure is usually possible within four to eight weeks.

Cheyletiellosis is caused by a relatively large mite, which sometimes can be seen even without a microscope. Often referred to as "walking dandruff," this also causes itching, but not usually as profound as with scabies. While *Cheyletiella* mites can survive

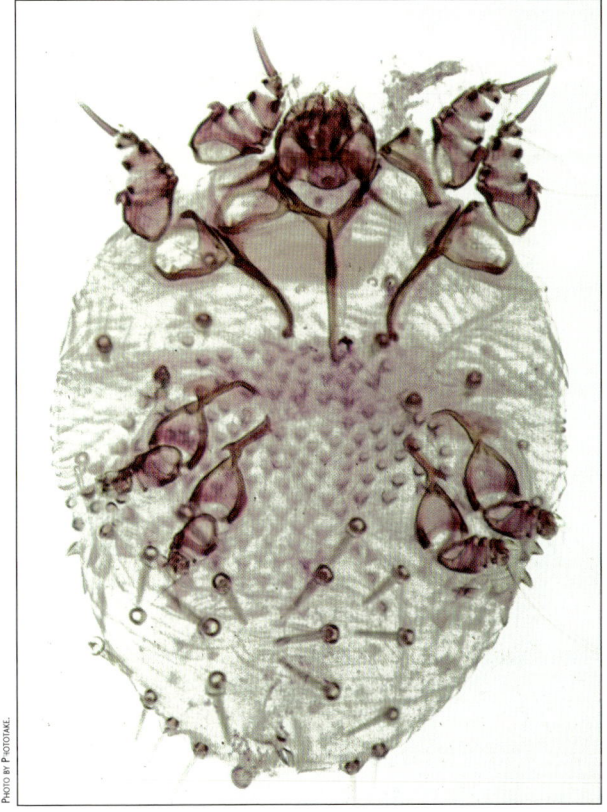

PHOTO BY PHOTOTAKE.

somewhat longer in the environment than scabies mites, they too are relatively easy to treat, being responsive to not only the medications used to treat scabies but also often to flea-control products.

Otodectes cynotis is the canine ear mite and is one of the more common causes of mange, especially in young dogs in shelters or pet stores. That's because the mites are typically present in large numbers and are quickly spread to nearby animals. The mites rarely do much harm but

Sarcoptes scabiei, commonly known as the "itch mite."

Micrograph of a dog louse, *Heterodoxus spiniger*. Female lice attach their eggs to the hairs of the dog. As the eggs hatch, the larval lice bite and feed on the blood. Lice can also feed on dead skin and hair. This feeding activity can cause hair loss and skin problems.

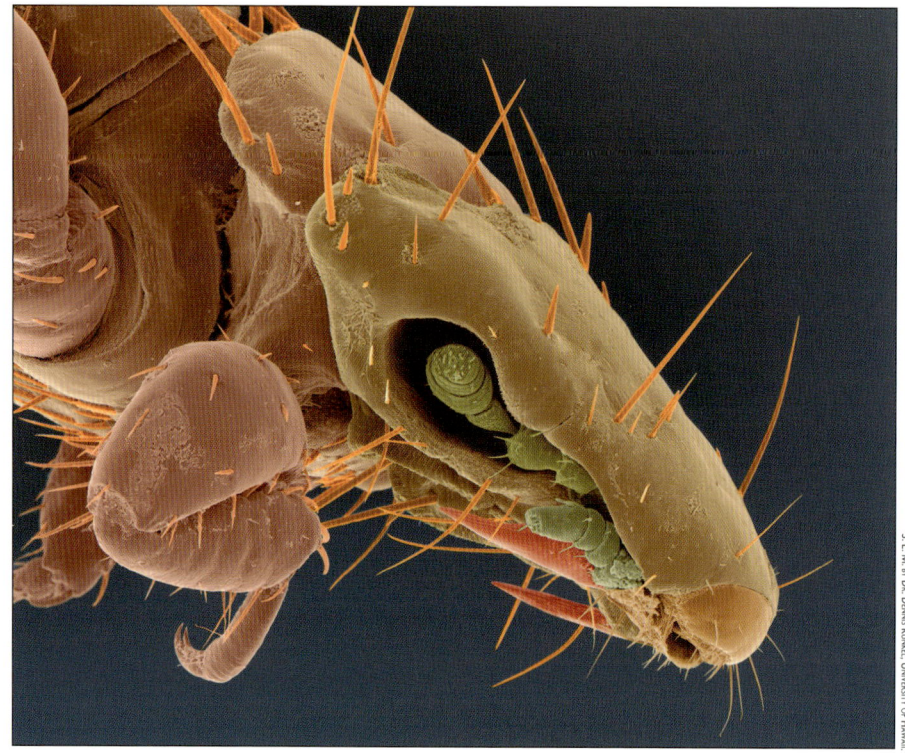

S. E. M. BY DR. DENNIS KUNKEL, UNIVERSITY OF HAWAII.

can be difficult to eradicate if the treatment regimen is not comprehensive. While many try to treat the condition with ear drops only, this is the most common cause of treatment failure. Ear drops cause the mites to simply move out of the ears and as far away as possible (usually to the base of the tail) until the insecticide levels in the ears drop to an acceptable level—then it's back to business as usual! The successful treatment of ear mites requires treating all animals in the household with a systemic insecticide, such as selamectin, or a combination of miticidal ear drops combined with whole-body flea-control preparations.

Demodicosis, sometimes referred to as red mange, can be one of the most difficult forms of mange to treat. Part of the problem has to do with the fact that the mites live in the hair follicles and they are relatively well shielded from topical and systemic products. The main issue, however, is that demodectic mange typically results only when there is some underlying process interfering with the dog's immune system.

Since *Demodex* mites are normal residents of the skin of

mammals, including humans, there is usually a mite population explosion only when the immune system fails to keep the number of mites in check. In young animals, the immune deficit may be transient or may reflect an actual inherited immune problem. In older animals, demodicosis is usually seen only when there is another disease hampering the immune system, such as diabetes, cancer, thyroid problems or the use of immune-suppressing drugs. Accordingly, treatment involves not only trying to kill the mange mites but also discerning what is interfering with immune function and correcting it if possible.

Chiggers represent several different species of mite that don't parasitize dogs specifically, but do latch on to passersby and can cause irritation. The problem is most prevalent in wooded areas in the late summer and fall. Treatment is not difficult, as the mites do not complete their life cycle on dogs and are susceptible to a variety of miticidal products.

MOSQUITOES

Mosquitoes have long been known to transmit a variety of diseases to people, as well as just being biting pests during warm weather. They also pose a real risk to pets. Not only do they carry deadly heartworms but recently there also has been much concern over their involvement with West Nile virus. While we can avoid heartworm with the use of preventive medications, there are no such preventives for West Nile virus. The only method of prevention in endemic areas is active mosquito control. Fortunately, most dogs that have been exposed to the virus only developed flu-like symptoms and, to date, there have not been the large number of reported deaths in canines as seen in some other species.

ILLUSTRATION BY PHOTOTAKE.

Illustration of Demodex folliculoram.

MOSQUITO REPELLENT

Low concentrations of DEET (less than 10%), found in many human mosquito repellents, have been safely used on dogs but, in these concentrations, probably give only about two hours of protection. DEET may be safe in these small concentrations, but since it is not licensed for use on dogs, there is no research proving its safety for dogs. Products containing permethrin give the longest-lasting protection, perhaps two to four weeks. As DEET is not licensed for use on dogs, and both DEET and permethrin can be quite toxic to cats, appropriate care should be exercised. Other products, such as those containing oil of citronella, also have some mosquito-repellent activity, but typically have a relatively short duration of action.

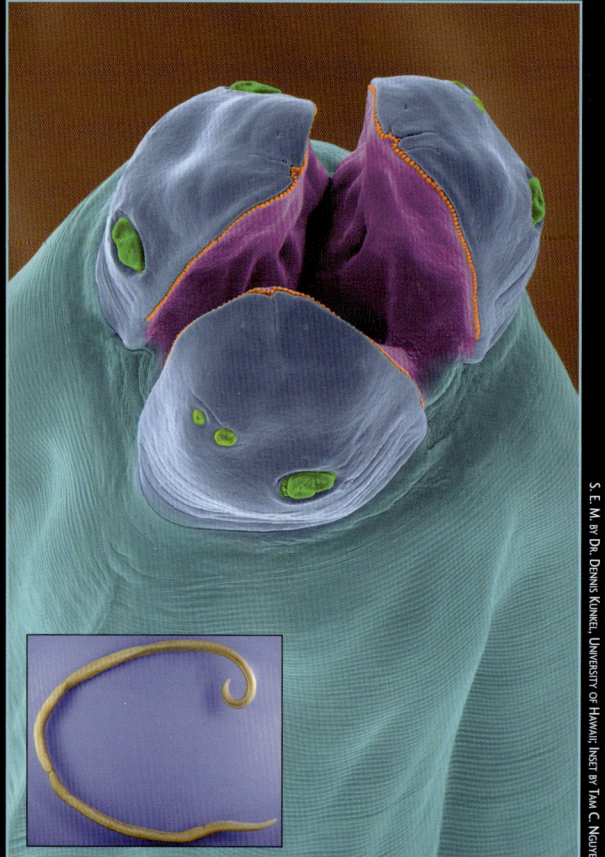

ASCARID DANGERS

The most commonly encountered worms in dogs are roundworms known as ascarids. *Toxascaris leonine* and *Toxocara canis* are the two species that infect dogs. Subsisting in the dog's stomach and intestines, adult round-worms can grow to 7 inches in length and adult females can lay in excess of 200,000 eggs in a single day.

In humans, visceral larval migrans affects people who have ingested eggs of *Toxocara canis*, which frequently contaminates children's sandboxes, beaches and park grounds. The round-worms reside in the human's stomach and intestines, as they would in a dog's, but do not mature. Instead, they find their way to the liver, lungs and skin, or even to the heart or kidneys in severe cases. Deworming puppies is critical in preventing the infection in humans, and young children should never handle nursing pups who have not been dewormed.

The ascarid roundworm *Toxocara canis,* showing the mouth with three lips. INSET: Photomicrograph of the roundworm *Ascaris lumbricoides.*

INTERNAL PARASITES: WORMS

ASCARIDS

Ascarids are intestinal round-worms that rarely cause severe disease in dogs. Nonetheless, they are of major public health significance because they can be transferred to people. Sadly, it is children who are most commonly affected by the para-site, probably from inadvertently ingesting ascarid-contaminated soil. In fact, many yards and children's sandboxes contain appreciable numbers of ascarid eggs. So, while ascarids don't bite dogs or latch onto their intestines to suck blood, they do cause some nasty medical condi-tions in children and are best eradicated from our furry friends. Because pups can start passing ascarid eggs by three weeks of age, most parasite-control programs begin at two weeks of age and are repeated every two weeks until pups are eight weeks

HOOKED ON ANCYLOSTOMA

Adult dogs can become infected by the bloodsucking nematodes we commonly call hookworms via ingesting larvae from the ground or via the larvae penetrating the dog's skin. It is not uncommon for infected dogs to show no symptoms of hookworm infestation. Sometimes symptoms occur within ten days of exposure. These symptoms can include bloody diarrhea, anemia, loss of weight and general weakness. Dogs pass the hookworm eggs in their stools, which serves as the vet's method of identifying the infestation. The hookworm larvae can encyst themselves in the dog's tissues and be released when the dog is experiencing stress.

Caused by an *Ancylostoma* species whose common host is the dog, cutaneous larval migrans affects humans, causing itching and lumps and streaks beneath the surface of the skin.

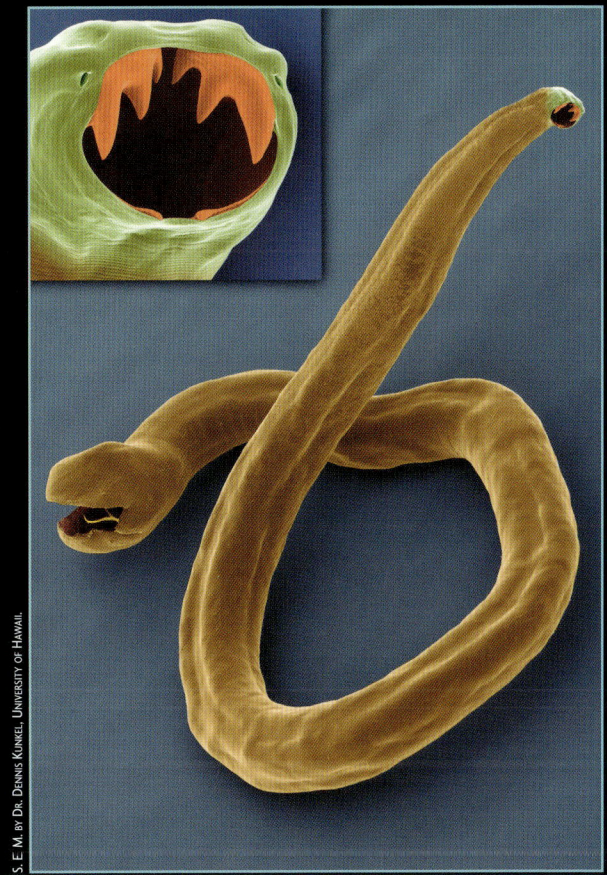

S. E. M. by Dr. Dennis Kunkel, University of Hawaii.

old. It is important to realize that bitches can pass ascarids to their pups even if they test negative prior to whelping. Accordingly, bitches are best treated at the same time as the pups.

HOOKWORMS

Unlike ascarids, hookworms do latch onto a dog's intestinal tract and can cause significant loss of blood and protein. Similar to ascarids, hookworms can be transmitted to humans, where they cause a condition known as cutaneous larval migrans. Dogs can become infected either by consuming the infective larvae or by the larvae's penetrating the skin directly. People most often get infected when they are lying on the ground (such as on a beach) and the larvae penetrate the skin. Yes, the larvae can penetrate through a beach blanket. Hookworms are typically susceptible to the same medications used to treat ascarids.

The hookworm *Ancylostoma caninum* infests the intestines of dogs. INSET: Note the row of hooks at the posterior end, used to anchor the worm to the intestinal wall.

WHIPWORMS

Whipworms latch onto the lower aspects of the dog's colon and can cause cramping and diarrhea. Eggs do not start to appear in the dog's feces until about three months after the dog was infected. This worm has a peculiar life cycle, which makes it more difficult to control than ascarids or hook-worms. The good thing is that whipworms rarely are transferred to people.

Some of the medications used to treat ascarids and hookworms are also effective against whipworms, but, in general, a separate treatment protocol is needed. Since most of the medications are effective against the adults but not the eggs or larvae, treatment is typically repeated in three weeks, and then often in three

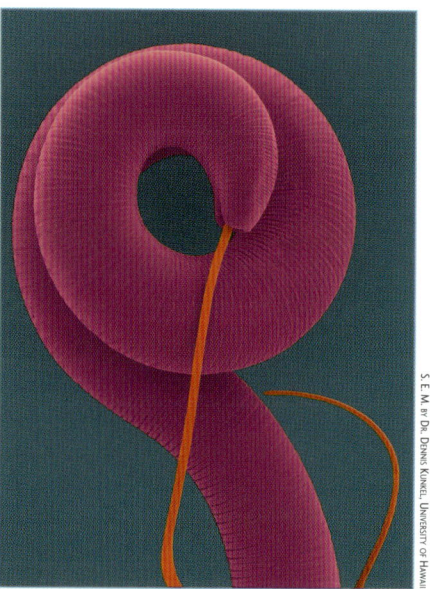

Adult whipworm, *Trichuris* sp., an intestinal parasite.

S. E. M. BY DR. DENNIS KUNKEL, UNIVERSITY OF HAWAII.

WORM-CONTROL GUIDELINES

- Practice sanitary habits with your dog and home.
- Clean up after your dog and don't let him sniff or eat other dogs' droppings.
- Control insects and fleas in the dog's environment. Fleas, lice, cockroaches, beetles, mice and rats can act as hosts for various worms.
- Prevent dogs from eating uncooked meat, raw poultry and dead animals.
- Keep dogs and children from playing in sand and soil.
- Kennel dogs on cement or gravel; avoid dirt runs.
- Administer heartworm preventives regularly.
- Have your vet examine your dog's stools at your annual visits.
- Select a boarding kennel carefully so as to avoid contamination from other dogs or an unsanitary environment.
- Prevent dogs from roaming. Obey local leash laws.

months as well. Unfortunately, since dogs don't develop resistance to whipworms, it is difficult to prevent them from getting rein-fected if they visit soil contaminated with whipworm eggs.

TAPEWORMS

There are many different species of tapeworm that affect dogs, but *Dipylidium caninum* is probably the most common and is spread by fleas. Flea larvae feed on organic debris and tapeworm eggs in the environment and, when a dog chews at himself and manages to ingest fleas, he might get a dose of tapeworm at the same time. The tapeworm then develops further in the intestine of the dog.

The tapeworm itself, which is a parasitic flatworm that latches onto the intestinal wall, is composed of numerous segments. When the segments break off into the intestine (as proglottids), they may accumulate around the rectum, like grains of rice. While this tapeworm is disgusting in its behavior, it is not directly communicable to humans (although humans can also get infected by swallowing fleas).

A much more dangerous tapeworm is *Echinococcus multilocularis*, which is typically found in foxes, coyotes and wolves. The eggs are passed in the feces and infect rodents, and, when dogs eat the rodents, the dogs can be infected by thousands of adult tapeworms. While the parasites don't cause many problems in dogs, this is considered the most lethal worm infection that people can get. Take appropriate precautions if you live in an area in which these tapeworms are found. Do not use mulch that may contain feces of dogs, cats or wildlife, and discourage your pets from hunting

wildlife. Treat these tapeworm infections aggressively in pets, because if humans get infected, approximately half die.

HEARTWORMS

Heartworm disease is caused by the parasite *Dirofilaria immitis* and is seen in dogs around the world. A member of the roundworm group, it is spread between dogs by the bite of an infected mosquito. The mosquito injects infective larvae into the dog's skin with its bite, and these larvae develop under the skin for a period of time before making their way to the heart. There they develop into adults, which grow and create blockages of the heart, lungs and major blood vessels there. They also start producing offspring (microfilariae),

A dog tapeworm proglottid (body segment).

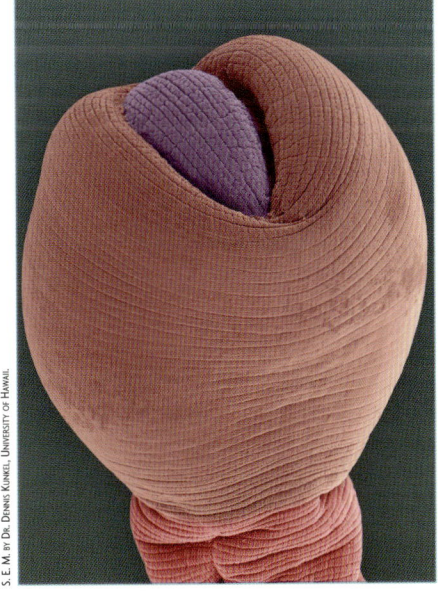

The dog tapeworm *Taenia pisiformis*.

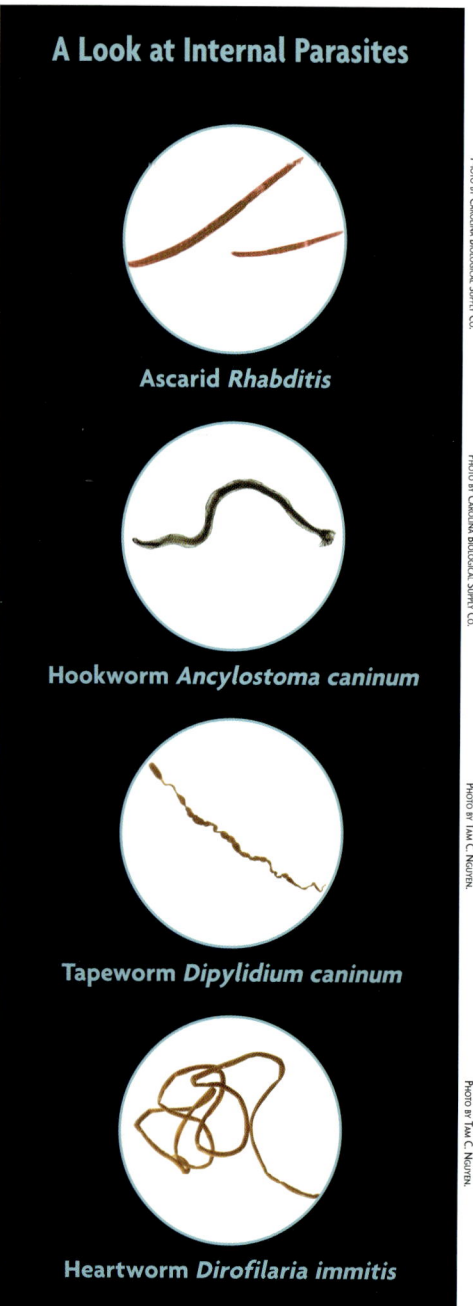

A Look at Internal Parasites

Ascarid *Rhabditis*

PHOTO BY CAROLINA BIOLOGICAL SUPPLY CO.

Hookworm *Ancylostoma caninum*

PHOTO BY CAROLINA BIOLOGICAL SUPPLY CO.

Tapeworm *Dipylidium caninum*

PHOTO BY TAM C. NGUYEN.

Heartworm *Dirofilaria immitis*

PHOTO BY TAM C. NGUYEN.

and these microfilariae circulate in the bloodstream, waiting to hitch a ride when the next mosquito bites. Once in the mosquito, the microfilariae develop into infective larvae and the entire process is repeated.

When dogs get infected with heartworm, over time they tend to develop symptoms associated with heart disease, such as coughing, exercise intolerance and potentially many other manifestations. Diagnosis is confirmed by either seeing the microfilariae themselves in blood samples or using immunologic tests (antigen testing) to identify the presence of adult heartworms. Since antigen tests measure the presence of adult heartworms and microfilarial tests measure offspring produced by adults, neither are positive until six to seven months after the initial infection. However, the beginning of damage can occur by fifth-stage larvae as early as three months after infection. Thus it is possible for dogs to be harboring problem-causing larvae for up to three months before either type of test would identify an infection.

The good news is that there are great protocols available for preventing heartworm in dogs. Testing is critical in the process, and it is important to understand the benefits as well as the limitations of such testing. All dogs six months of age or older that have not been on continuous heartworm-preventive medication

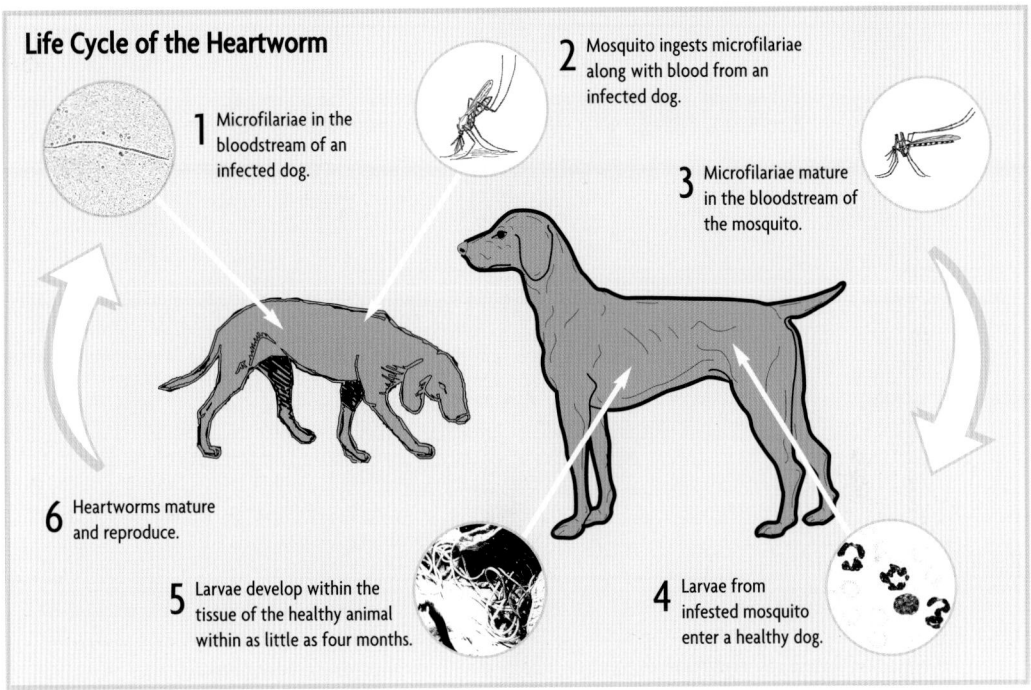

Life Cycle of the Heartworm

1 Microfilariae in the bloodstream of an infected dog.

2 Mosquito ingests microfilariae along with blood from an infected dog.

3 Microfilariae mature in the bloodstream of the mosquito.

4 Larvae from infested mosquito enter a healthy dog.

5 Larvae develop within the tissue of the healthy animal within as little as four months.

6 Heartworms mature and reproduce.

should be screened with microfilarial or antigen tests. For dogs receiving preventive medication, periodic antigen testing helps assess the effectiveness of the preventives. The American Heartworm Society guidelines suggest that annual retesting may not be necessary when owners have absolutely provided continuous heartworm prevention. Retesting on a two- to three-year interval may be sufficient in these cases. However, your veterinarian will likely have specific guidelines under which heartworm preventives will be prescribed, and many prefer to err on the side of safety and retest annually.

It is indeed fortunate that heartworm is relatively easy to prevent, because treatments can be as life-threatening as the disease itself. Treatment requires a two-step process that kills the adult heartworms first and then the microfilariae. Prevention is obviously preferable; this involves a once-monthly oral or topical treatment. The most common oral preventives include ivermectin (not suitable for some breeds), moxidectin and milbemycin oxime; the once-a-month topical drug selamectin provides heartworm protection in addition to flea, some types of tick and other parasite controls.

THE **ABC**s OF
Emergency Care

Abrasions

Clean wound with running water or 3% hydrogen peroxide. Pat dry with gauze and spray with antibiotic. Do not cover.

Animal Bites

Clean area with soap and saline solution or water. Apply pressure to any bleeding area. Apply antibiotic ointment. Identify biting animal and contact the vet.

Antifreeze Poisoning

Induce vomiting and take dog to the vet.

Bee Sting

Remove stinger and apply soothing lotion or cold compress; give antihistamine in proper dosage.

Bleeding

Apply pressure directly to wound with gauze or towel for five to ten minutes. If wound does not stop bleeding, wrap wound with gauze and adhesive tape.

Bloat/Gastric Torsion

Immediately take the dog to the vet or emergency clinic; phone from car. No time to waste.

Burns

Chemical: Bathe dog with water and pet shampoo. Rinse in saline solution. Apply antibiotic ointment.

Acid: Rinse with water. Apply one part baking soda, two parts water to affected area.

Alkali: Rinse with water. Apply one part vinegar, four parts water to affected area.

Electrical: Apply antibiotic ointment. Seek veterinary assistance immediately.

Choking

If the dog is on the verge of collapsing, wedge a solid object, such as the handle of a screwdriver, between molars on one side of mouth to keep mouth open. Pull tongue out. Use long-nosed pliers or fingers to remove foreign object. Do not push the object down the dog's throat. For small or medium dogs, hold dog upside down by hind legs and shake firmly to dislodge foreign object.

Chlorine Ingestion

With clean water, rinse the mouth and eyes. Give dog water to drink; contact the vet.

Constipation

Feed dog 2 tablespoons bran flakes with each meal. Encourage drinking water. Mix 1/4-teaspoon mineral oil in dog's food. Contact vet if persists longer than 24 hours.

Diarrhea

Withhold food for 12 to 24 hours. Feed dog anti-diarrheal with eyedropper. When feeding resumes, feed one part boiled hamburger, one part plain cooked rice, 1/4 to 3/4 cup four times daily. Contact vet if persists longer than 24 hours.

Dog Bite

Snip away hair around puncture wound; clean with 3% hydrogen peroxide; apply tincture of iodine. Identify biting dog and call the vet. If wound appears deep, take the dog to the vet.

Frostbite

Wrap the dog in a heavy blanket. Warm affected area with a warm bath for ten minutes. Red color to skin will return with circulation; if tissues are pale after 20 minutes, contact the vet.

Use a portable, durable container large enough to contain all items.

Heat Stroke
Submerge the dog (up to his muzzle) in cold water; if no response within ten minutes, contact the vet.

Hot Spots
Mix 2 packets Domeboro® with 2 cups water. Saturate cloth with mixture and apply to hot spots for 15–30 minutes. Apply antibiotic ointment. Repeat every six to eight hours.

Poisonous Plants
Wash affected area with soap and water. Cleanse with alcohol. For foxtail/grass, apply antibiotic ointment. Contact vet if plant was ingested.

Rat Poison Ingestion
Induce vomiting. Keep dog calm, maintain dog's normal body temperature (use blanket or heating pad). Get to the vet for antidote.

Shock
Keep the dog calm and warm; call for veterinary assistance.

Snake Bite
If possible, bandage the area and apply pressure. If the area is not conducive to bandaging, use ice to control bleeding. Get immediate help from the vet.

Tick Removal
Apply flea and tick spray directly on tick. Wait one minute. Using tweezers or wearing plastic gloves, grasp the tick's body firmly and pull out. Apply antibiotic ointment.

Vomiting
Restrict water intake; offer a few ice cubes. Withhold food for next meal. Contact vet if vomiting persists longer than 24 hours.

DOG OWNER'S FIRST-AID KIT
- ❏ Gauze bandages/swabs
- ❏ Adhesive and non-adhesive bandages
- ❏ Antibiotic powder
- ❏ Antiseptic wash
- ❏ Hydrogen peroxide 3%
- ❏ Antibiotic ointment
- ❏ Lubricating jelly
- ❏ Rectal thermometer
- ❏ Nylon muzzle
- ❏ Scissors and forceps
- ❏ Eyedropper
- ❏ Syringe
- ❏ Anti-bacterial/fungal solution
- ❏ Saline solution
- ❏ Antihistamine
- ❏ Cotton balls
- ❏ Nail clippers
- ❏ Screwdriver/pen knife
- ❏ Flashlight
- ❏ Emergency phone numbers

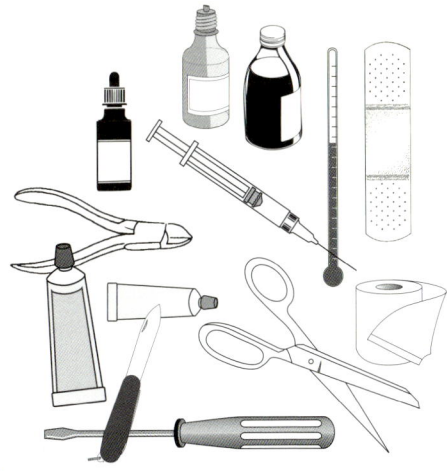

BLACK AND TAN COONHOUND

Ch. Southchases Warrior Princess, a top winner at the turn of the millennium, shown winning one of her Bests in Show at Onondaga Kennel Club in 2000, handled by Vic Capone.

Is dog showing in your blood? Are you excited by the idea of gaiting your handsome Black and Tan Coonhound around the ring to the thunderous applause of an enthusiastic audience? Are you certain that your beloved Black and Tan Coonhound is flawless? You are not alone! Every loving owner thinks that his dog has no faults, or too few to mention. No matter how many times an owner reads the breed standard, he cannot find any faults in his aristocratic companion dog. If this sounds like you, and if you are considering entering your Black and Tan Coonhound in a dog show, here are some basic questions to ask yourself:

- Did you purchase a "show-quality" puppy from the breeder?
- Is your puppy old enough to show?
- Does the puppy exhibit correct show type for his breed?
- Does your puppy have any disqualifying faults?
- Is your Black and Tan Coonhound registered with the American Kennel Club or United Kennel Club?
- How much time do you have to devote to training, grooming, conditioning and exhibiting your dog?
- Do you understand the rules and regulations of a dog show?
- Do you have time to learn how to show your dog properly?
- Do you have the financial resources to invest in showing your dog?
- Will you show the dog yourself or hire a professional handler?
- Do you have a vehicle that can accommodate your weekend trips to the dog shows?

Success in the show ring requires more than a pretty face, a waggy tail and a pocketful of liver. Even though dog shows can be exciting and enjoyable, the sport of conformation makes great demands on the exhibitors and the dogs. Winning exhibitors live for their dogs, devoting time and money to their dogs' presentation, conditioning and training. Very few novices, even those with good dogs, will find themselves in the winners' circle, though it does happen. Don't be disheartened, though. Every exhibitor began as a novice and worked his way up to the Group ring. It's the "working your way up" part that you must keep in mind.

Best of Breed at Westminster in 2003 was Ch. Southchases Can You Do Magic, bred and owned by Lynda Webb and Stan Bielowicz. The judge was Susan St. John Brown.

FOR MORE INFORMATION...

For reliable up-to-date information about registration, dog shows and other canine competitions, contact one of the national registries by mail or via the Internet.

American Kennel Club
5580 Centerview Dr., Raleigh, NC 27606-3390
www.akc.org

United Kennel Club
100 E. Kilgore Road, Kalamazoo, MI 49002
www.ukcdogs.com

Canadian Kennel Club
89 Skyway Ave., Suite 100, Etobicoke, Ontario M9W 6R4, Canada
www.ckc.ca

Assuming that you have purchased a puppy of the correct type and quality for showing, let's begin to examine the world of showing and what's required to get started. Although the entry fee into a dog show is nominal, there are lots of other hidden costs involved with "finishing" your Black and Tan Coonhound, that is, making him a champion. Things like equipment, travel, training and conditioning all cost money. A more serious campaign will include fees for a professional handler, boarding, cross-country travel and advertising. Top-winning show dogs can represent

a very considerable investment—over $100,000 has been spent in campaigning some dogs. (The investment can be less, of course, for owners who don't use professional handlers.)

Many owners, on the other hand, enter their "average" Black and Tan Coonhounds in dog shows for the fun and enjoyment of it. Dog showing makes an absorbing hobby, with many rewards for dogs and owners alike. If you're having fun, meeting other people who share your interests and enjoying the overall experience, you likely will catch the "bug." Once the dog-show bug bites, its effects can last a lifetime; it's certainly much better than a deer tick! Soon you will be envisioning yourself in the center ring at the Westminster Kennel Club Dog Show in New York City, competing for the prestigious Best

in Show cup. This magical dog show is televised annually from Madison Square Garden, and the victorious dog becomes a celebrity overnight.

AKC CONFORMATION SHOWING

GETTING STARTED

Visiting a dog show as a spectator is a great place to start. Pick up the show catalog to find out what time your breed is being shown, who is judging the breed and in which ring the classes will be held. To start, Black and Tan Coonhounds compete against other Black and Tan Coonhounds, and the winner is selected as Best of Breed by the judge. This is the procedure for each breed. At a group show, all of the Best of Breed winners go on to compete for Group One in their respective

SHOW POTENTIAL

How possible is it to predict how your ten-week-old puppy will eventually do in the show ring? Most show dogs reach their prime at around three years of age, when their bodies are physically mature and their coats are in "full bloom." Experienced breeders, having watched countless pups grow into Best of Breed winners, recognize the glowing attributes that spell "show potential." When selecting a puppy for show, it's best to trust the breeder to recommend which puppy will best suit your aspirations. Some breeders recommend starting with a male puppy, which likely will be more "typey" than his female counterpart.

group. For example, all Best of Breed winners in a given group compete against each other; this is done for all seven groups. Finally, all seven group winners go head to head in the ring for the Best in Show award.

What most spectators don't understand is the basic idea of conformation. A dog show is often referred as a "conformation" show. This means that the judge should decide how each dog stacks up (conforms) to the breed standard for his given breed: how well does this Black and Tan Coonhound conform to the ideal representative detailed in the standard? Ideally, this is what happens. In reality, however, this ideal often gets

slighted as the judge compares Black and Tan Coonhound #1 to Black and Tan Coonhound #2. Again, the ideal is that each dog is judged based on his merits in comparison to his breed standard, not in comparison to the other dogs in the ring. It is easier for judges to compare dogs of the same breed to decide which they think is the better specimen; in the Group and Best in Show ring, however, it is very difficult to compare one breed to another, like apples to oranges. Thus the dog's conformation to the breed standard—not to mention advertising dollars and good handling—is essential to success in conformation shows. The dog described in the standard (the standard for each AKC breed is written and approved by the breed's national parent club and then submitted to the AKC for

From teeth to tail, the judge performs a hands-on evaluation of each dog, feeling for correct body construction and soundness.

closer and closer to the ideal with each litter.

Another good first step for the novice is to join a dog club. You will be astonished by the many and different kinds of dog clubs in the country, with about 5,000 clubs holding events every year. Most clubs require that prospective new members present two letters of recommendation from existing members. Perhaps you've made some friends visiting a show held by a particular club and you would like to join that club. Dog clubs may specialize in a single breed, like a local or regional Black and Tan Coonhound club, or in a specific pursuit, such as obedience, tracking or hunting tests. There are all-breed clubs for all dog enthusiasts; they sponsor special training days, seminars on topics like grooming or handling or lectures on breeding or canine genetics. There are also clubs that specialize in certain types of dogs, like herding dogs, hunting dogs, companion dogs, etc.

A parent club is the national organization, sanctioned by the AKC, which promotes and safeguards its breed in the country. The American Black and Tan Coonhound Club can be contacted on the Internet at www.abtcc.com. The parent club holds an annual national specialty show, usually in a different city each year, in which many of the country's top

ON THE MOVE

The truest test of a dog's proper structure is his gait, the way the dog moves. The American Kennel Club defines gait as "the pattern of footsteps at various rates of speed, each pattern distinguished by a particular rhythm and footfall." That the dog moves smoothly and effortlessly indicates to the judge that the dog's structure is well made. From the four-beat gallop, the fastest of canine gaits, to the high-lifting hackney gait, each breed varies in its correct gait; not every breed is expected to move in the same way. Each breed standard defines the correct gait for its breed and often identifies movement faults, such as toeing in, side-winding, over-reaching or crossing over.

approval) is the perfect dog of that breed, and breeders keep their eye on the standard when they choose which dogs to breed, hoping to get

The relationship between dog and handler is vital in determining how the entry will "stack up" in the show ring.

dogs, handlers and breeders gather to compete. At a specialty show, only members of a single breed are invited to participate. There are also group specialties, in which all members of a group are invited. For more information about dog clubs in your area, contact the AKC at www.akc.org on the Internet or write them at their Raleigh, NC address.

OTHER TYPES OF COMPETITION

In addition to conformation shows, the AKC holds a variety of other competitive events. Obedience trials, agility trials and tracking trials are open to all breeds, while hunting tests, field trials, lure coursing, herding tests and trials, earthdog tests and coonhound events are limited to specific breeds or groups of breeds. The Junior Showmanship Program is offered to aspiring young handlers and their dogs, and the Canine Good Citizen® Program is an all-around good-behavior test open to all dogs, pure-bred and mixed.

OBEDIENCE TRIALS

Mrs. Helen Whitehouse Walker, a Standard Poodle fancier, can be credited with introducing obedience trials to the United States. In the 1930s she designed a series of exercises based on those of the Associated Sheep,

Best Bred by Exhibitor at the Eukanuba Invitational in 2002, here is Ch. Rockytop Dynasty of Sumar.

Police, Army Dog Society of Great Britain. These exercises were intended to evaluate the working relationship between dog and owner. Since those early days of the sport in the US, obedience trials have grown more and more popular, and now more than 2,000 trials each year attract over 100,000 dogs and their owners. Any dog registered with the AKC, regardless of neutering or other disqualifications that would preclude entry in conformation competition, can participate in obedience trials.

There are three levels of difficulty in obedience competition. The first (and easiest) level is the Novice, in which dogs can earn the Companion Dog (CD) title. The intermediate level is the Open level, in which the Companion Dog Excellent (CDX) title is awarded. The advanced level is the Utility level, in which dogs compete for the Utility Dog (UD) title. Classes at each level are further divided into "A" and "B," with "A" for beginners and "B" for those with more experience. In order to win a title at a given level, a dog must earn three "legs." A "leg" is accomplished when a dog scores 170 or higher (200 is a perfect score). The scoring system gets a little trickier when you understand that a dog must score more than 50% of the points available for each exercise in order to actually earn the points. Available points for each exercise range between 20 and 40.

A dog must complete different exercises at each level of obedi-

DRESS THE PART

It's a dog show, so don't forget your costume. Even though the show is about the dog, you also must play your role well. You have been cast as the "dog handler" and you must smartly dress the part. Solid colors make a nice complement to the dog's coat, but choose colors that contrast. You don't want to be wearing a solid color that blends mostly or entirely with the major or only color of your dog. Whether the show is indoors or out, you still must dress properly. You want the judge to perceive you as being professional, so polish, polish, polish! And don't forget to wear sensible shoes; remember, you have to gait around the ring with your dog.

ence. The Novice exercises are the easiest, with the Open and finally the Utility levels progressing in difficulty. Examples of Novice exercises are on- and off-lead heeling, a figure-8 pattern, performing a recall (or come), long sit and long down and standing for examination. In the Open level, the Novice-level exercises are required again, but this time without a leash and for longer durations. In addition, the dog must clear a broad jump, retrieve over a jump and drop on recall. In the Utility level, the exercises are quite difficult, including executing basic commands based on hand signals, following a complex heeling pattern, locating articles based on scent discrimination and completing jumps at the handler's direction.

Once he's earned the UD title, a dog can go on to win the prestigious title of Utility Dog Excellent (UDX) by winning "legs" in ten shows. Additionally, Utility Dogs who win "legs" in Open B and Utility B earn points toward the lofty title of Obedience Trial Champion (OTCh.). Established in 1977 by the AKC, this title requires a dog to earn 100 points as well as 3 first places in a combination of Open B and Utility B classes under 3 different judges. The "brass ring" of obedience competition is the AKC's National Obedience Invitational. This is an exclusive competition for only the cream of the obedience crop. In order to qualify for the invitational, a dog must be ranked in either the top 25 all-breeds in obedience or in the top 3 for his breed in obedience. The title at stake here is that of National Obedience Champion (NOC).

RALLY OBEDIENCE

In 2005 the AKC began a new program called Rally obedience, and soon this exciting agility spin-off began sweeping the US. This is a less formal activity yet titles are awarded. There are four levels of competition. Novice, Advanced, Excellent and Advanced/Excellent. The dog and handler do a series of exercises designed by the judge and are timed. The handlers are encouraged to talk to their dog as they work through the course.

Ch. Dach Lair's Tribute to 3 Kings, winner of the 2006 AKC Coonhound World Championship, with (L to R) owners Chirpie Birdsall and Dr. David Birdsall, handler Kathy Shorter, judge Don Smith and Maxine Smith.

participate in obedience or agility also do well in Rally. While most of the first Rally titles have gone to seasoned obedience dogs, it's encouraging that some newcomers have also earned awards. Rally is a good way for a beginner to start out in obedience, and we hope that it will become a stepping stone to the obedience world, and we will see many more dogs and owners coming into the ring.

AGILITY TRIALS

Agility trials became sanctioned by the AKC in August 1994, when the first licensed agility trials were held. Since that time, agility certainly has grown in popularity by leaps and bounds, literally! The AKC allows all registered breeds (including Miscellaneous Class breeds) to participate, providing the dog is 12 months of age or older. Agility is designed so that the handler demonstrates how well the dog can work at his side. The handler directs his dog through, over, under and around an obstacle course that includes jumps, tires, the dog walk, weave poles, pipe tunnels, collapsed tunnels and more. While working his way through the course, the dog must keep one eye and ear on the handler and the rest of his body on the course. The handler runs along with the dog, giving verbal and hand signals to guide the dog through the course.

In the ring, the judge will note how the dog conforms to the ideal set forth in the breed standard, which is what the dog is being compared to, not the other dogs.

The judge evaluates each team on how well it executes one continuous performance over the whole course. The team works on its own as soon as the judge gives the order to begin. Handlers develop their own style in working with their dogs, using a combination of body language and hand signals as well as verbal commands. Faster and more accurate are desirable, though each team must work at its own pace. Signs are set up around the ring to indicate which exercise (or combination of exercises) is required. Working closely around the course, the team heels from one sign to the next, performing the various exercises. There are 50 exercises to choose from, varying in complexity and difficulty.

The dogs love this and it shows by their animation and energy. Many of the dogs who

The first organization to promote agility trials in the US was the United States Dog Agility Association, Inc. (USDAA). Established in 1986, the USDAA sparked the formation of many member clubs around the country. To participate in USDAA trials, dogs must be at least 18 months of age.

The USDAA and AKC both offer titles to winning dogs, although the exercises and requirements of the two organizations differ. Agility Dog (AD), Advanced Agility Dog (AAD) and Master Agility Dog (MAD) are the titles offered by the USDAA, while the AKC offers Novice Agility (NA), Open Agility (OA), Agility Excellent (AX) and Master Agility Excellent (MX). Beyond these four AKC titles,

dogs can win additional titles in "jumper" classes: Jumper with Weave Novice (NAJ), Open (OAJ) and Excellent (MXJ). The ultimate title in AKC agility is MACH, Master Agility Champion. Dogs can continue to add number designations to the MACH title, indicating how many times the dog has met the title's requirements (MACH1, MACH2 and so on).

Agility trials are a great way to keep your dog active, and they will keep you running, too! You should join a local agility club to learn more about the sport. These clubs offer sessions in which you can introduce your dog to the various obstacles as well as training classes to prepare him for competition. In no time, your dog will be climbing A-frames, crossing the dog walk and flying over hurdles, all

While the Black and Tan is not a small dog, in some instances he might be evaluated on a table, so it should be introduced during training.

EXPRESS YOURSELF

The most intangible of all canine attributes, expression speaks to the character of the breed, attained by the combined features of the head. The shape and balance of the dog's skull, the color and position of the eyes and the size and carriage of the head mingle to produce the correct expression of the breed. A judge may approach a dog and determine instantly whether the dog's face portrays the desired impression for the breed, conveying nobility, intelligence and alertness among other specifics of the breed standard.

Showing that he's an all-around top dog, Ch. Dach Lair's Tribute to 3 Kings also won the National Grand Show Championship at the UKC's 2006 Autumn Oaks competition under judge Gene Allhands.

with you right beside him. Your heart will leap every time your dog jumps through the hoop—and you'll be having just as much (if not more) fun!

COMPETITION HUNTING

Breed clubs as well as hunting and field trial clubs hold competition hunting, events sponsored by registries such as the UKC and AKC. The purpose of the hunt is to tree as many squirrels as possible within a given amount of time. Squirrel-hunting dogs that earn the number of points required by whichever club sponsors the

event are awarded titles such as Squirrel Champion or Grand Squirrel Champion. Championship titles are difficult to achieve and require a great deal of time and effort in training. Hunts take place mostly in the southern states and are held throughout the year; participants often travel great distances to attend the hunt.

NITE HUNTS

Nite hunts are also sponsored by different registries and involve four Coonhound hunts lasting for two hours. There are four hunts sponsored at a time, and the events are judged by the sponsoring clubs. Titles are given such as Nite Champion and Grand Nite Champion.

COON HUNTS

Various registries hold coon hunts throughout the year. At the hunt the Coonhound is scored on how fast and how many coons he can tree in a given amount of time. A bench show is another type of event sponsored by the United Kennel Club, and the Coonhound is judged much the same way that hogs and sheep are judged at a livestock show. Sanctioned Coonhound events have grown into international competitions; one event sponsored by the United Kennel Club was held in Paris. Over 100 dogs from 20 states competed for the top title and prize money. The Coonhound was scored on being the first to tree a raccoon.

THE UNITED KENNEL CLUB

Most sporting and hunting dogs have many opportunities to compete in both conformation and other events. A glance at the United Kennel Club (UKC) website (www.ukcdogs.com) tells us that the UKC is America's second oldest and second largest all-breed dog registry, attracting around 250,000 registrations each year. Chauncey Z. Bennett founded the UKC in 1898 with an aim to support the "total dog," meaning a dog that possesses quality in physical conformation and performance alike. With that

AMERICA'S ALTERNATIVE: THE UNITED KENNEL CLUB

The United Kennel Club (UKC) defines itself as follows: "With 300,000 registrations annually, the United Kennel Club is the world's largest performance dog registry and second oldest all-breed registry in the United States. Founded in 1898, the UKC has supported the 'Total Dog' philosophy through its events and programs for over a century. As a departure from registries that place emphasis on a dog's looks, UKC events are designed for dogs that look and perform equally well." Professional handlers are not permitted in UKC shows, and the club goes on to state, "At UKC dog shows, the emphasis is on the dog, not the show."

True to its aim of promoting the "Total Dog," the UKC hosts conformation events as well as a multitude of performance events, including obedience trials; agility trials; field trials, water races, nite hunts and bench shows for coonhound breeds; hunting tests for retrieving breeds; Beagle events, including hunts and bench shows; squirrel and coon events and bench shows for Cur and Feist; weight pulling and more. There is junior handling program to encourage the next generation of up-and-coming responsible owners and participants in the dog sport.

For more information, visit the UKC online at www.ukcdogs.com.

in mind, the UKC sponsors competitive events that emphasize this "total dog" aspect. Along with traditional conformation shows, the UKC's performance events encompass just about every skill that one could imagine in a dog! These performance events include obedience, agility, coonhound trials, water races, hunting tests designed for specific types of dog (retrievers, Beagles, curs and feists, etc.) and much more. The website goes on to say, "Essentially, the UKC world of dogs is a working world. That's the way founder Chauncey Bennett designed it, and that's the way it remains today."

What many think of as traditional "dog shows" are more formally known as conformation shows. These are competitive events in which dogs are evaluated based on their conformation to their breed's standard, which is the official written description of the ideal representative of that breed. The standards recognized by the UKC are either adopted from those of Europe's canine registry, the Fédération Cynologique Internationale (FCI) or submitted by the American breed club and then revised and adopted by the UKC. At many shows, handlers will receive verbal "critiques" of their dogs; these critiques may always be requested if not given automatically. This critique details a dog's

comparison to the breed standard, and the judge also will explain why he placed each dog as he did.

UKC dog shows may be held for one breed only, several breeds or all breeds. UKC shows are arranged differently from the conformation shows of other organizations. Entries are restricted by age, and you cannot show your dog in a class other than his correct age class. When you compete for championship points, you may enter Puppy (6-12 months), Junior (1-2 years), Senior (2-3 years) or Adult (3 years and older). You may also enter the Breeder/Handler Class, where dogs of all ages compete, but the dog must be handled by his breeder or a member of the breeder's immediate family. The winners of each class compete for Best Male or Best Female. These two dogs then compete for Best of Winners; the dog who is given this award will go on to compete for Best of Breed. Best of Breed competition includes the Best of Winners and dogs that have earned Champion and Grand Champion titles. Earning Best Male or Best Female, as long as there is competition, is considered a "major."

Once a dog has earned 3 "majors" and accumulated 100 points, he is considered a UKC champion. What this means is that the dog is now ready to compete for the title of Grand

Champion, which is equivalent to an AKC championship. To earn the Grand Champion title, a dog must compete with a minimum of two other dogs who are also champions. The dog must win this class, called the Champion of Champions class, five times under three different judges. In rare breeds, it is difficult to assemble a class of champions, so the UKC Grand Champion title is truly a prestigious one. Once a dog has earned the Grand Champion title, he can continue to compete for Top Ten, but there are no further titles to earn. "Top Ten" refers to the ten dogs in each breed that have won the most points in a given year. These dogs compete in a Top Ten invitational competition annually.

The breeds recognized by the UKC are divided into groups. The Black and Tan Coonhound competes in the Scenthound–Group 2, which consists of dogs of similar utility and/or heritage. Depending on the show-giving club, Group competition may or may not be offered. A group must have a minimum of five breeds entered in order for Group competition to take place. If Group competition is offered, Best in Show consists of the Group winners. If there is no Group competition, then all Best of Breed dogs go into the ring at the same time to compete for Best in Show. This can be a large number

of dogs and thus can be very interesting, to say the least!

Aside from the variations already presented, UKC shows differ from other dog shows in one very significant way: no professional handlers are allowed to show dogs, except for those dogs they own themselves. UKC shows create an atmosphere that is owner-friendly, relaxed and genuinely fun. Bait in the ring is allowed at the discretion of the judge, but throwing the bait, dropping it on the floor or other "handler tricks" will get an owner excused from the ring in a hurry.

In addition to dog shows, the UKC offers many more venues for dogs and their owners, in keeping with its mission of promoting the "total dog." UKC obedience events test the training of dogs as they perform a

The Black and Tan Coonhound is an agile breed that is capable of great success in many athletic types of competition. Here, Ch. Rockytop Mountain Moonshine does a retrieve over the high jump.

series of prescribed exercises at the commands of their handlers. There are several levels of competition, ranging from basic commands such as "sit," "come" and "heel," to advanced exercises like scent discrimination and directed retrieves over jumps, based on the dog's level of accomplishment. The classes are further delineated by the experience of the handler.

CLASSES AT UNITED KENNEL CLUB DOG SHOWS

The Regular classes, for all dogs who are not Champions or Grand Champions, are divided by sex (and variety) with four winners selected by the judge. Champions and Grand Champions are judged separately, with one winner in each class. The Regular classes are broken down into the following:

Puppy Class: Male and female puppies, from six months to one year of age.

Junior Class: Male and female dogs, from one year to under two years of age.

Senior Class: Male and female dogs, from two years of age to under three years of age.

Adult Class: Male and female dogs, three years of age and older.

Breeder/Handler Class: Male and female dogs, six months of age and older, handled by the breeder of record or a member of the breeder's immediate family.

UKC obedience differs from AKC obedience in many respects. Even at the most basic levels, the dogs are expected to "honor" other dogs who are working. In other words, the "honoring" dog must be placed in a down/stay while his owner leaves the ring and moves out of sight. The dog must remain in the down/stay position while the working dog goes through the heeling exercises.

Agility events are fast-paced exercises in which the handler directs his dog through a course involving tunnels, sway bridges, jumps and other obstacles in a race against the clock. The dogs are scored according to the manner in which they negotiate the obstacles and the time elapsed to complete the course. UKC agility is very similar to AKC agility; clubs often will offer both AKC and UKC agility events (not on the same day).

Weight-pull events give certain dogs the opportunity to perform a function that comes naturally to them, and one that they obviously enjoy. Of course, not all dogs are talented or willing weight-pullers, but many are. Basically, a dog is placed in a harness that is attached to a weighted vehicle, which the dog pulls a prescribed distance. The weighted vehicles operate either on wheels, on snow or on a rail system. The dogs are scored on how much weight they can pull;

these scores are based on the proportion of the dog's body weight to the amount of weight pulled. Weight pulling requires quite a bit of training, although even the smallest breeds are allowed to participate. The most important equipment required for weight pulling is a properly fitting harness. Once the handler has dropped the harness or traces, the dog is on his own. The handler can neither bait nor call the dog and cannot touch the dog until he has crossed the finish line and the judge has signaled a "pull."

Hunting with hounds is an American tradition that still enjoys immense popularity. The UKC's competitive hound programs offer events for coonhound enthusiasts belonging to over 1,300 clubs throughout the United States and Canada. In fact, the UKC's coonhound events have up to 17,000 coonhounds entered annually and rank as the largest sporting-dog events of any kind in the world!

The bottom line is this: there is so much to do with your dog that it can be hard to decide which event to try! Whatever you choose to do with your dog, it will take training, dedication and a willingness to work with your dog to achieve a common goal, a partnership between you and your dog. There is nothing more pleasing than to watch a handler and dog performing at a high level, whether it is the show ring or the field. There is something for everyone and every dog in the world of dog "showing." Dog showing should really be called "competing with your dog." You are not restricted to the traditional "dog show" and may find that your "show dog" excels in other areas as well or instead.

JUNIOR SHOWMANSHIP

Junior Showmanship competitions are excellent training grounds for the up-and-coming generation of exhibitors. Junior handlers learn by grooming, handling and training their dogs, and the quality of a junior's presentation of the dog (and himself) is evaluated by a licensed judge. Young handlers are encouraged to join dog clubs, take classes and seek advice from seasoned exhibitors.

American Kennel Club Junior Showmanship (conformation) is open to youngsters between the ages of 9 and 18. Junior handlers are also encouraged to participate in AKC companion and performance events, in which they compete in regular classes. The AKC's National Junior Organization promotes the dog sport to young people, and the AKC also offers a Junior Scholarship.

The United Kennel Club's Junior Program welcomes young handlers to experience the dog sport through participation in performance events and traditional conformation showing. Juniors from ages 2 to 18 are recognized for their achievements, with emphasis on sportsmanship, adherence to the rules and regulations and responsible ownership and training.

BLACK AND TAN COONHOUND

You chose your dog because something clicked the minute you set eyes on him. Or perhaps it seemed that the dog selected you and that's what clinched the deal. Either way, you are now investing time and money in this dog, a true pal and an outstanding member of the family. Everything about him is perfect—well, almost perfect. Remember, he is a dog! For that matter, how does he think *you're* doing?

UNDERSTANDING THE CANINE MINDSET

For starters, you and your dog are on different wavelengths. Your dog is similar to a toddler in that

both live in the present tense only. A dog's view of life is based primarily on cause and effect, which is similar to the old saying, "Nothing teaches a youngster to hang on like falling off the swing." If your dog stumbles down a flight of three steps, the next time he will try the Superman approach and fling himself off the top one!

Your dog makes connections based on the fact that he lives in the present, so when he is doing something and you interrupt to dispense praise or a correction, a connection, positive or negative, is made. To the dog, that's like one plus one equals two! In the same sense, it's also easy to see that when your timing is off, you will cause an incorrect connection. The one-plus-one way of thinking is why you must never scold a dog for behavior that took place an hour, 15 minutes or even 5 seconds ago. But it is also why, when your timing is perfect, you can teach him to do all kinds of wonderful things—as soon as he has made that essential connection. What helps the process is his desire to please you and to have your approval.

It is important to encourage proper behavior from the very beginning of your Black and Tan's life with you.

There are behaviors we admire in dogs, such as friendliness and obedience, as well as those behaviors that cause problems to a varying degree. The dog owner who encounters minor behavioral problems is wise to solve them promptly or get professional help. Bad behaviors are not corrected by repeatedly shouting "No" or getting angry with the dog. Only the giving of praise and approval for good behavior lets your dog understand right from wrong. The longer a bad behavior is allowed to continue, the harder it is to overcome. A responsible breeder is often able to help. Each dog is unique, so try not to compare your dog's behavior with your neighbor's dog or the one you had as a child.

Have your veterinarian check the dog to see whether a behavior problem could have a physical cause. An earache or toothache, for example, could be the reason for a dog to snap at you if you were to touch his head when putting on his leash. A sharp correction from you would only increase the behavior. When a physical basis is eliminated, and if the problem is not something you understand or can cope with, ask for the name of a behavioral specialist, preferably one who is familiar with the Black and Tan Coonhound. Be sure to keep the breeder informed of your progress.

UNDERSTANDING HOW YOUR DOG TICKS

Dogs do not run on human emotions like love, guilt or spite. They operate on trust and loyalty, or faithfulness, and those are worthy alternatives to what we call love. Dogs don't understand any human language, but they can learn to make connections if all corrections and praise are immediate. If your dog demolished your rug while you were out, that's not guilt you're seeing, but a reaction to your anger. He doesn't know why you're angry, but he knows the boss isn't happy. Dogs are pack animals. They have always lived in a cooperative society. Your dog retains that pack instinct, requiring a leader. You now have that job and the responsibility that goes along with it.

Many things, such as environment and inherited traits, form the basic behavior of a dog, just as in humans. You also must factor into his temperament the purpose for which your dog was originally bred. The major obstacle lies in the dog's inability to explain his behavior to us in a way that we understand. The one thing you should not do is to give up and abandon your dog. Somewhere a misunderstanding has occurred but, with help and patient understanding on your part, you should be able to work out the majority of bothersome behaviors.

Interaction between two dogs should always be monitored, although overly physical behavior does not necessarily constitute aggression.

AGGRESSION

"Aggression" is a word that is often misunderstood and is sometimes even used to describe what is actually normal canine behavior. For example, it's normal for puppies to growl when playing tug-of-war. It's puppy talk. There are different forms of dog aggression, but all are degrees of dominance, indicating that the dog, not his master, is (or thinks he is) in control. When the dog feels that he (or his control of the situation) is threatened, he will respond. The extent of the aggressive behavior varies with individual dogs. It is not at all pleasant to see bared teeth or to hear your dog growl or snarl, but these are signs of behavior that, if left uncorrected, can become extremely dangerous. A word of warning here: never challenge an aggressive dog. He is unpredictable and therefore unreliable to approach.

Nothing gets a "hello" from strangers on the street quicker than walking a puppy, but people should ask permission before potting your dog so you can tell him to sit in order to receive the admiring pats. If a hand comes down over the dog's head and he shrinks back, ask the person to bring their hand up, underneath the pup's chin. Now you're correcting strangers, too! But if you don't, it could make your dog afraid of strangers, which in turn can lead to fear-biting. Socialization prevents much aggression before it rears its ugly head.

The body language of an aggressive dog about to attack is clear. The dog will have a hard, steady stare. He will try to look as big as possible by standing stiff-legged, pushing out his chest, keeping his ears up and holding his tail up and steady. The hackles on his back will rise so that a ridge of hairs stands up. This posture may include the curled lip, snarl and/or growl, or he may be silent. He looks, and definitely is, very dangerous.

This dominant posture is seen in dogs that are territorially aggressive. Deliverymen are constant victims of serious bites from such dogs. Territorial aggression is the reason you should never, ever, try to train a puppy to be a watchdog. It can escalate into this type of behavior over which you will have no control.

All forms of aggression must be taken seriously and dealt with immediately. If signs of aggressive behavior continue, or grow worse, or if you are at all unsure about how to deal with your dog's behavior, get the help of a professional.

Uncontrolled aggression, sometimes called "irritable aggression," is not something for the pet owner to try to solve. If you cannot solve your dog's dangerous behavior with professional help, and you (quite rightly) do not wish to keep a canine time-bomb in your home, you will have some important decisions to make. Aggressive dogs often cannot be rehomed successfully, as they are dangerous and unreliable in their behavior. An aggressive dog should be dealt with only by someone who knows exactly the situation that he is getting into and has the experience, dedication and ideal living environment to attempt rehabilitating the dog, which often is not possible. In these cases, the dog ends up having to be humanely put down. Making a decision about euthanasia is not an easy undertaking for anyone, for any reason, but you cannot pass on to another home a dog that you know could cause harm.

A milder form of aggression is the dog's guarding anything that he perceives to be his—his food dish, his toys, his bed and/or his crate. This can be prevented if you take firm control from the start. The young puppy can and should be taught that his leader will share, but that certain rules apply. Guarding is mild aggression only in the beginning stages, and it will worsen and become dangerous if you let it.

Don't try to snatch anything away from your puppy. Bargain for the item in question so that you can positively reinforce him when he gives it up. Punishment only results in worsening any aggressive behavior.

Many dogs extend their guarding impulse toward items they've stolen. The dog figures, "If I have it, it's mine!" (Some ill-behaved kids have similar tendencies.) An angry confrontation will only increase the dog's aggression. (Have you ever watched a child have a tantrum?) Try a simple distraction first, such as tossing a toy or picking up his leash for a walk. If that doesn't work, the best

ONE BITE TOO MANY

It's natural for puppies to bite in play, but you must teach your puppy that this is unacceptable in human circles. Relax your hand, say "No bite" and offer him a toy. An adolescent dog is testing his dominance and will bite as a way of disobeying you. If not stopped in puppyhood, you will end up with an adult dog that will bite aggressively. All adult biting should be considered serious and dealt with by a professional.

While a child will surely enjoy puppy kisses, a nip from an overwhelmed pup will not evoke the same reaction, so be sure to supervise interaction between the two.

way to handle the situation is with basic obedience. Show the dog a treat, followed by calm, almost slow-motion commands: "Come. Sit. Drop it. Good dog," and then hand over the cheese! That's one example of positive-reinforcement training.

Children can be bitten when they try to retrieve a stolen shoe or toy, so they need to know how to handle the dog or to let an adult do it. They may also be bitten as they run away from a dog, in either fear or play. The dog sees the child's running as reason for pursuit, and even a friendly young puppy will nip at the heels of a runaway. Teach the kids not to run away from a strange dog and when to stop overly exciting play with their own puppy.

Fear-biting is yet another aggressive behavior. A fear biter gives many warning signals. The dog leans away from the

approaching person (sometimes hiding behind his owner) with his ears and tail down, but not in submission. He may even shiver. His hackles are raised, his lips curled. When the person steps into the dog's "flight zone" (a circle of 1 to 3 feet surrounding the dog), he attacks. Because of the fear factor, he performs a rapid attack-and-retreat. Because it is directed at a person, vets are often the victims of this form of aggression. It is frightening, but discovering and eliminating the cause of the fright will help overcome the dog's need to bite. Early socialization again plays a strong role in the prevention of this behavior. Again, if you can't cope with it, get the help of an expert.

SEPARATION ANXIETY
Any behaviorist will tell you that separation anxiety is the most common problem about which pet

---

DOMINANCE
Dogs are born with dominance skills, meaning that they can be quite clever in trying to get their way. The "follow-me" trot to the cookie jar is an example. The toy dropped in your lap says "Play with me." The leash delivered to you along with an excited look means "Take me for a walk." These are all good-natured dominant behaviors. Ask your dog to sit before agreeing to his request and you'll remain "top dog."

owners complain. It is also one of the easiest to prevent. Unfortunately, a behaviorist usually is not consulted until the dog is a stressed-out, neurotic mess. At that stage, it is indeed a problem that requires the help of a professional.

Training the puppy to the fact that people in the house come and go is essential in order to avoid this anxiety. Leaving the puppy in his crate or a confined area while family members go in and out, and stay out for longer and longer periods of time, is the basic way to desensitize the pup to the family's frequent departures. If you are at home most of every day, make it a point to go out for at least an hour or two whenever possible.

How you leave is vital to the dog's reaction. Your dog is no fool. He knows the difference between sweats and business suits, jeans and dresses. He sees you pat your pocket to check for your wallet, open your briefcase, check that you have your cell phone or pick up the car keys. He knows from the hurry of the kids in the morning that they're off to school until afternoon. Lipstick? Aftershave lotion? Lunch boxes? Every move you make registers in his sensory perception and memory. Your puppy knows more about your departures than you do. You can't get away with a thing!

Before you got dressed, you checked the dog's water bowl and

Your hound will be much happier if he is safe and warm in the house during your absence rather than chained outdoors.

his supply of toys (including a long-lasting chew toy), and turned the radio on low. You will leave him in what he considers his "safe" area, not with total freedom of the house. If you've invested in child safety gates, you can be reasonably sure that he'll remain in the designated area. Don't give him access to a window where he can watch you leave the house. If you're leaving for an hour or two, just put him into his crate with a safe toy.

Now comes the test! You are ready to walk out the door. Do not give your Black and Tan Coonhound a big hug and a fond farewell. Do not drag out a long goodbye. Those are the very things that jump-start separation anxiety. Toss a biscuit into the dog's area, call out "So long, pooch" and close the door.

You're gone. The chances are that the dog may bark a couple of times, or maybe whine once or twice, and then settle down to enjoy his biscuit and take a lovely nap, especially if you took him for a nice long walk after breakfast. As he grows up, the barks and whines will stop because it's an old routine, so why should he make the effort?

When you first brought home the puppy, the come-and-go routine was intermittent and constant. He was put into his crate with a tiny treat. You left (silently) and returned in 3 minutes, then 5, then 10, then 15, then half an hour, until finally you could leave without a prob- lem and be gone for 2 or 3 hours. If, at any time in the future, there's a "separation" problem, refresh his memory by going back to that basic training.

Now comes the next most important part—your return. Do not make a big production of

The tendency to dig varies from dog to dog. When it occurs, it is a behavior you need to discourage or at least control.

coming home. "Hi, poochie" is as grand a greeting as he needs. When you've taken off your hat and coat, tossed your briefcase on the hall table and glanced at the mail, and the dog has settled down from the excitement of seeing you "in person" from his confined area, then go and give him a warm, friendly greeting. A potty trip is needed and a walk would be appreciated, since he's been such a good dog.

DIGGING

Digging is another natural and normal doggy behavior. Wild canines dig to bury whatever food they can save for later to eat. (And you thought *we* invented the doggy bag!) Burying bones or toys is a primary cause to dig. Dogs also dig to get at interesting little underground creatures like moles and mice. In the summer, they dig to get down to cool earth. In winter, they dig to get beneath the cold surface to warmer earth.

The solution to the last two is easy. In the summer, provide a bed that's up off the ground and placed in a shaded area. In winter, the dog should either be indoors to sleep or given an adequate insulated doghouse outdoors. To understand how natural and normal this is you have only to consider the Nordic breeds of sled dog who, at the end of the run, routinely dig a bed for themselves in the snow. It's the nesting instinct. How often have you seen your dog go round and round in circles, pawing at his blanket or bedding before flopping down to sleep?

Domesticated dogs also dig to escape, and that's a lot more dangerous than it is destructive. A dog that digs under the fence is the one that is hit by a car or becomes lost. A good fence to protect a digger should be set 10 to 12 inches below ground level, and every fence needs to be routinely checked for even the smallest openings that can become possible escape routes.

Catching your dog in the act of digging is the easiest way to stop it, because your dog will make the "one-plus-one" connection, but digging is too often a solitary occupation, something the lonely dog does out of boredom. Catch your young puppy in the act and put a stop to it before you have a yard full of craters. It is more difficult to stop if your dog sees you gardening. If you can dig, why can't he? Because you say so, that's why! Some dogs are excavation experts, and some dogs never dig. However, when it comes to any of these instinctive canine behaviors, never say "never."

BARKING

Here's a big, noisy problem! Telling a dog he must never bark is like telling a child not to speak! Consider how confusing it must be to your dog that you are using

The Black and Tan Coonhound has a distinctive bark that comes in handy when on the hunt. You may not want your dog to be as vocal in the home, so do not encourage barking from the start.

your voice (which is your form of barking) to teach him when to bark and when not to! That is precisely the reason not to "bark back" when the dog's barking is annoying you (or your neighbors). Try to understand the scenario from the dog's viewpoint. He barks. You bark. He barks again, you bark again. This "conversation" can go on forever!

The first time your adorable little puppy said "Yip" or "Yap, you were ecstatic. His first word! You smiled, you told him how smart he was—and you allowed him to do it. So there's that one-plus-one thing again, because he will understand by your happy reaction that "Mr. Alpha loves it when I talk." Ignore his barking in the beginning, and allow it, but don't encourage barking during play. Instead, use the "put a toy in it" method to tone it down. Add a very soft "Quiet" as you hand off the toy. If the barking continues, stand up straight, fold your arms and turn your back on the dog. If he barks, you won't play, and you should follow the same rule for all undesirable behavior during play.

Dogs bark in reaction to sounds and sights. Another dog's bark, a person passing by or even just rustling leaves can set off a barker. If someone coming up your driveway or to your door provokes a barking frenzy, use the saturation method to stop it. Have several friends come and go every three or four minutes over as long a period of time as they can spare (it could take a couple of hours). Attach about a foot of rope to the dog's collar and have very small treats handy. Each time a car pulls up or a person approaches, let the dog bark once (grab the rope if you need to physically restrain him), say "Okay, good dog," give him a treat and make him sit. "Okay" is the release command. It lets the dog know that he has alerted you and tells him that you are now in charge. That person leaves and the next arrives, and so on and so on until everyone— especially the dog—is bored and the barking has stopped. Don't

forget to thank your friends. Your neighbors, by the way, may be more than willing to assist you in this parlor game.

Excessive barking outdoors is more difficult to keep in check because, when it happens, he is outside and you are probably inside. A few warning barks are fine, but use the same method to tell him when enough is enough. You will have to stay outside with him for that bit of training.

There is one more kind of vocalizing which is called "idiot barking" (from idiopathic, meaning of unknown cause). It is usually rhythmic or a timed series of barks. Put a stop to it immediately by calling the dog to come. This form of barking can drive neighbors crazy and commonly occurs when a dog is left outside at night or for long periods of time during the day. He is completely and thoroughly bored! A change of scenery may help, such as relocating him to a room indoors when he is used to being outside. A few new toys or different dog biscuits might be the solution. If he is left alone and no one can get home during the day, a noontime walk with a local dog-sitter would be the perfect solution.

FOOD-RELATED PROBLEMS

We're not talking about eating, diets or nutrition here, we're talking about bad habits. Face it. All dogs are beggars. Food is the motivation for everything we want our dogs to do and, when you combine that with their innate ability to "con" us in order to get their way, it's a wonder there aren't far more obese dogs in the world.

Who can resist the bleeding-heart look that says "I'm starving," or the paw that gently pats your knee and gives you a knowing look, or the whining "please" or even the total body language of a perfect sit beneath the cookie jar. No one who professes to love his dog can turn down the pleas of his clever canine's performances every time. One thing is for sure, though: definitely do not allow begging at the table. Family meals do not include your dog.

Control your dog's begging habit by making your dog work for his rewards. Ignore his begging when you can. Utilize the obedience commands you've taught your dog. Use "Off" for the pawing. A sit or even a long down will interrupt the whining. His reward in these situations is definitely not a treat! Casual verbal praise is enough. Be sure all members of the family follow the same rules.There is a different type of begging that does demand your immediate response and that is the appeal to be let (or taken) outside! Usually that is a quick paw or small whine to get your attention, followed by a race to the door. This type of begging needs your quick attention and approval. Of course, a really smart

dog will soon figure out how to cut you off at the pass and direct you to that cookie jar on your way to the door! Some dogs are always one step ahead of us.

Stealing food is a problem only if you are not paying attention. A dog can't steal food that is not within his reach. Leaving your dog in the kitchen with the roast beef on the table is asking for trouble. Nothing idiopathic about this problem, though perhaps a little idiotic! Putting cheese and crackers on the coffee table also requires a watchful eye to stop the thief in his tracks. The word to use (one word, remember, even if it's two words pronounced as one) is "Leave it!" Instead of preceding it with yet another "No," try using a guttural sound like "Aagh!" That sounds more like a warning growl to the dog and therefore has instant meaning.

Canine thieves are in their element when little kids are carrying cookies in their hands! Your dog will think he's been exceptionally clever if he causes a child to drop a cookie. Bonanza! The easiest solution is to keep dog and children separated at snack time. You must also be sure that the children understand that they must not tease the dog with food—his or theirs. Your dog does not mean to bite the kids, but when he snatches at a tidbit so near the level of his mouth, it can result in an unintended nip.

Acetaminophen 59
Activities 99
Adenovirus 110
Adult dog
—adoption 81
—health 105
—training 80-81
Aggression 58, 82, 112, 148-149
Agility 99
Aging 105
Air travel 78
Allergies 62
Alpha role 88
American Black andTan Association 18
American Black and Tan Coonhound Club 29
—specialty show 29
American Black and Tan Fox and Coonhound 11
American Foxhound 13
American Heartworm Society 127
American Kennel Club 18, 28, 36, 131
—conformation showing 133-140
Ancylostoma braziliense 123
Ancylostoma caninum 123, 126
Annual vet exams 105
Antifreeze 47
Appetite loss 105
Ascarid 122, 123
Ascaris lumbricoides 122
Attention 23, 89, 91, 96
Bark scorpion 107
Barking 21, 23, 153
—controlling 154
Bathing 67-68
Bawl 23
Bedding 42, 49, 86
Behavioral problems 147
Behavioral specialist 147, 150
Birdsall, Dr. David and Chirpie 137
Birdsong, Col. George Lawrence F. 17
Biting 149-150
Blindness 24
Bloodhound 12-14
Boarding 79
Body language 82, 87, 95, 148, 155
Body temperature 108
Bones 43, 62

Boone, Daniel 12
Booster shots 46
Bordetella 110
Bordetella bronchiseptica 111
Boredom 23, 153
Borrelia burgdorferi 110
Borreliosis 111
Bowls 40
Breed standard 28-29, 31, 39
—faults 28
Breeder 31, 37
—selection 36, 38, 101
Breeding 25, 29
Brooke, Robert 13
Browning, Mary Lou 14
Browning, Robert 18
Browning's Black Beauty 12
Browning's Dixie 18
Browning's Mindy 10
Browning's Rambling Joe 8, 14
Browning's Trooper 8
Brucker, Jeff 16
Brushing 67
Buchanan, Dr. 17
Cabral, Martin 132
Cancer 112
Canine cough 110
Capone, Vic 130
Car travel 76-77
Cat 55, 59
Cataract 25
Cats 23
Chaney's Black George 11
Chew toys 42-43, 54, 85-86
Chewing 42, 53
Cheyletiella mite 119
Chiggers 121
Children 23, 48, 50, 53, 55, 82, 150, 155
Cognitive dysfunction 106
Collars 44, 76, 90
Colostrum 46
Come 52, 95
Commands 91-98
—potty 87
—practicing 92, 94
Competition hunting 140
Consistency 51, 54, 57, 90
Coon hunts 141
Coonskin cap 12
Core vaccines 111
Coronavirus 110-111
Correction 89, 146
Counter surfing 57
Crate 40, 48-49, 56, 77, 85, 151

—pads 42
—training 42, 83
Crockett, Davy 12
Crying 49, 56, 86
Ctenocephalides canis 114
Cystitis 106
Dach Lair's Tribute to 3 Kings 137, 140
Dangers in the home 45, 47
Dental
—care 73, 103, 106
—health 72, 105
DEET 121
Demodex mite 121
Demodicosis 120-121
Designer Southern Tradition 19
Diet 61-62
—making changes 61
—senior 63
Digging 56, 152
Dipylidium caninum 124, 126
Dirofilaria immitis 125, 126, 127
Discipline 52, 88-89
Distemper 110-111
Dog flea 114
Dominance 92, 148-150
Down 55, 86, 92, 95
Down/stay 94
Drifters 21
Drooling 67
Dry baths 68
Dunham, Orville O. 19
Ear
—cleaning 71
—mite 71, 119-120
Echinococcus multilocularis 125
Ectropion 26
Eggs 62
Emergency care 128-129
English Foxhound 13
Escaping 153
Estrus 112, 113
Excessive thirst 64, 106
Exercise 65
—pen 84, 85
External parasites 114-121
Family meeting the puppy 47
Fear period 50
Fear-biting 148, 150
Feeding 58, 61-62
—adult 62
—schedule 61
Fenced yard 23, 46, 153
First night in new home 48

Fleas 114, 115, 116
Food 61-62, 85
—allergies 62
—bowls 40
—loss of interest in 105
—raw 62
—rewards 81, 90, 97
—types 61-62
Food guarding 57
Food stealing 155
Foxhound 13-17
Foxtails 72
Genetic testing 101
Giardia 110
Gould, Edwin Dr. 18
Grand Mere Lassie 19
Grass eating 66
Grinder for nails 70
Grooming 67-68, 70, 73
Guarding 149
Health 24, 47
—adult 105
—insurance for pets 109
—journal 47
—puppy 37, 101
—senior dog 106
Heart disease 106
Heartworm 103, 125, 126, 127
Heat cycle 112, 113
Heel 96-97
Height 29
Hematuria 106
Henry, Dr. Thomas 17
Hepatitis 110-111
Heterodoxus spiniger 120
Hicks' Black Bandit 13
Hicks' Dynamite Dan 17
Hicks, Gene 17
Hip dysplasia 25
Homemade toys 44
Hookworm 123, 126
Hot spot 111
House-training 40, 42, 83, 86-87
—puppy needs 84
—schedule 85, 88
Hunting 21, 38-39, 99
Identification 74-76
Infectious diseases 109-111
Insects 107
Insurance 109
Internal parasites 122-127
Irritable aggression 149
Ixodes dammini 117-118
Jumping up 54, 86
Karlena's Musical C Note 19

Kidney problems 106
Leash 45, 90
—pulling on 97
Leptospirosis 110-111
Lifespan 105
Litter box 55
Liver 62
Lost dog 76
Louse 120
Loyalty 147
Luttrell's Tiger 8
Lyme disease 111
Mammary cancer 112
McAteer, Davin 16
Meat 62
Microchip 75
Midge 8
Milk 62
Minerals 63
Mites 71, 119, 120, 121
Mosquitoes 121, 125, 127
Mounting 112
Murray, Mignon 19
Nail clipping 69-70
Name 91, 96
Nesting behavior 112
Neutering 103, 111-113
Night blindness 24
Nipping 53, 55, 149
Nite hunts 140-141
Non-core vaccines 111
Obedience 23, 93
—classes 98
—trials 98
Off 55, 57, 86
Okay 93, 97, 154
Ole Rock 10
Original purpose 10
Orthopedic Foundation for
  Animals 26
Other dogs 112
Other pets 23, 55, 82
Otodectes cynotis 119
Outdoor safety 46, 153
Ovariohysterectomy 112-113
Pack animals 51, 147
Paper-training 83, 86-87
Parainfluenza 110-111
Parasites
—control 103
—external 114-121
—internal 122-127
Parvovirus 110-111
Pedigree 39
Plants 44
Playtime 95

Poisons 44, 46-47, 59
Positive reinforcement 48, 89,
  91, 146, 150
Possessive behavior 58, 149
Powell, Donald R. 19
Practicing commands 92, 94
Praise 81, 89-90, 98, 146-147
Preventive care 101, 105-106
Problem behavior 147
Proglottid 125
Progressive retinal atrophy
  24
Prostate problems 112
Pseudocyesis 112
Punishment 24, 57, 88-89, 149
Puppy
—common problems 53
—establishing leadership 80
—feeding 61
—first night in new home 48
—health 37-38, 101
—kindergarten training class
  90
—meeting the family 47
—needs 84
—personality 103
—proofing 44-45
—selection 36-38, 80, 101
—show quality 37, 39
—socialization 49
—supplies for 40
—teething 53
—temperament 41
—training 51, 80, 90
Pyotraumatic dermatitis 111
Quiet 154
Rabies 110-111
Rawhide 43
Retinal photoreceptors 24
Rewards 81, 88, 89-90, 97
—food 89
Rhabditis 126
Roaming 112
Rockytop Dynasty of Sumar
  136
Rockytop Mountain Moonshine
  143
Rockytop Winnie the Pooh 16
Rollridge Anna Bell 11
Rope toys 44
Roundworm 122, 123, 126
Safety 41, 44-45, 59, 77, 84, 86, 95
—in the car 77
—outdoors 46
—yard 153
Sarcoptes scabiei 119

Scabies 119
Scent attraction 87
Schedule 85
Schenker, Bill 15
Schenker's Black Jet 15
Senior dog 105
—diet 63
—health 106
Separation anxiety 150
Sex differences 39
Shedding 67
Shorter, Kathy 137
Show quality 39
Sit 91
Sit/stay 93
Skin conditions 111
Smokey 14
Socialization 39, 48-49, 51, 91,
  103, 148, 150
Soft toys 43
Southchases Brave Heart 132
Southchases Can You Do Magic
  131
Southchases Warrior Princess
  130
Spaying 103, 111-113
Spider 107
Spot bath 68
St. Hubert Hound 9, 11
Standard 39
Stay 93, 97
Stealing food 155
Straddlers 21
Stray dog 76
Stress 99
Supervision 23, 52-53, 86
Surgery 113
Table scraps 62
Taenia pisiformis 125
Tapeworm 124, 125, 126
Tattoo 75-76
Teeth 73, 103, 105
Teething period 53
Temperament 22-23, 41, 147
—evaluation 103
Temperature
—taking your dog's 108
Territorial aggression 148
Testicular cancer 112
Therapy dog 99
Thirst 64, 106
Tick-borne diseases 117
Ticks 117-118
Timing 87, 90, 95, 146
Toxascaris leonine 122
Toxins 44, 46-47, 59, 62

Toxocara canis 122
Toys 42-43, 54, 85-86
Tracheobronchitis 110
Tracking 99
Training 23, 57
—basic principles of 80, 90
—commands 91
—consistent 51, 54
—crate 42, 83
—early 51
—importance of timing 87, 95,
  146
—practice 92
—puppy 90
—tips 52
Travel 41, 77-78
Traverse Hill Flashdance 19
Traverse Hill Gypsy Woman 17
Treats 48, 81, 89-90
—weaning off in training 97
Trichuris sp. 124
Tricks 99
United Kennel Club 11, 18, 28,
  36, 131, 141-145
Urinary tract problems 106
Urine marking 112
Vaccinations 46-47, 50, 103, 109
—issues regarding proper
  protocol 111
Veterinarian 25, 43-44, 47, 103,
  105, 147
—selection of 106
Veterinary insurance 109
Veterinary specialties 108
Visiting the litter 36
Vitamin A toxicity 62
Vitamins 63
Watchdog 22
Water 64, 85
—bowls 40
—increased intake 64, 106
West Nile virus 121
Whining 49, 56, 86
Whipworm 124
William the Conqueror 12
Worm control 124
Wolf 112
Wyeast Why Not 20
Yard 46

My Black and Tan Coonhound

PUT YOUR PUPPY'S FIRST PICTURE HERE

Dog's Name _____

Date _____ Photographer _____